# Kobe

## and the

# New
# Lakers
# Dynasty

# Kobe
## and the
# New
# Lakers
# Dynasty

MARK HEISLER

Triumph Books and colophon are registered trademarks of Random House, Inc.

Library of Congress Cataloging-in-Publication Data
Heisler, Mark.
  Kobe and the new Lakers dynasty / Mark Heisler.
    p. cm.
  ISBN 978-1-60078-350-0
  1. Bryant, Kobe, 1978– 2. African American basketball players—United States—
Biography. 3. Los Angeles Lakers (Basketball team) I. Title.
  GV884.B794H45 2009
  796.323092—dc22
  [B]
                                2009033903

This book is available in quantity at special discounts for your group or organization. For further information, contact:
  **Triumph Books**
  542 South Dearborn Street
  Suite 750
  Chicago, Illinois 60605
  (312) 939-3330
  Fax (312) 663-3557
  www.triumphbooks.com

Printed in U.S.A.
ISBN: 978-1-60078-350-0

Design by Patricia Frey

Photos courtesy of Getty Images

# Contents

# Acknowledgments

With much of this material coming from the two editions of my book *Madmen's Ball*, I have already thanked the people who contributed so much to my understanding of the Lakers.

Nevertheless, I would be remiss if I didn't thank Jerry West, Magic Johnson, Phil Jackson, Mitch Kupchak, and John Black, who have been helpful for decades, and all the beat writers from all the newspapers, from the great Doug Krikorian and the one and only Mitch Chortkoff to Mike Bresnahan and Brad Turner, who chased the Lakers up hill and over dale and made the entire adventure so much fun.

Thanks also to Mitch Rogatz, my publisher, and Don Gulbrandsen, my editor, at Triumph Books, and, as always, to the loves of my life, Loretta and Emily.

—Mark Heisler
Northridge, California

*Alone at last: Kobe with his fourth Larry O'Brien Trophy...and his first Finals MVP trophy.*

# Kobe Diem

This was how it always was, either the best of times or the worst of times. If Paris was the City of Lights and New York was the city that never sleeps, Los Angeles was the celebrities' city, where stars went to become stars, and the Lakers were the stars' stars.

In Magic Johnson's heyday in the '80s, Capitol Records president Joe Smith called him the biggest star in town after watching him leave a room full of gaping movie stars at lunch at Le Dome on the Sunset Strip.

Magic's time was long over now, and Kobe Bryant's had finally come. This mother of all Laker parades, celebrating their 2009 title, was Bryant's fourth but his first without Shaquille O'Neal. O'Neal had stolen the show while they won their three titles in 2000, 2001, and 2002, being named the MVP of all three Finals and dominating the victory celebrations with his stage-ready emcee personality. In any reckoning of greatness, it was always noted that Kobe won his first three titles with Shaq. No one ever said Shaq was diminished by winning his first three with Kobe.

Suddenly, it was as if Kobe had gone from zero to four. Making it as official as it gets, Hannah Storm of ESPN's *SportsCenter* announced the day after the Lakers won their title in Orlando: "Kobe Bryant can now be placed on the list of the greatest players of all time."

That was certainly nice for Bryant, but he had been that good for years—and even better in the days when he didn't have as much help and had to be all he could be—while being derided as selfish, arrogant, and so on.

Economic times being what they were in the summer of 2009, the Los Angeles City Council wouldn't pay the costs for a parade, obliging private donors to step up. Of course, with a long waiting list for $2,500-per-game courtside seats, the Lakers' season-ticket holders could have come up with it with the cash they had on them. So it was on, after all, with Mayor Antonio Villaraigosa, the rising star of local politics, all over the Lakers now.

Usually blasé L.A. citizens reacted as if they had spent all seven years since the last Laker parade lining up for this one. Thousands lined the two-and-a-half-mile route from Staples Center to the Coliseum, bearing signs like "Kobe Diem," a takeoff on *carpe diem*, Latin for "seize the day."

The Coliseum, where the ceremony was held, was jammed to its 96,000 capacity, with thousands more who couldn't get in milling around outside. Wrote *LA Weekly*'s Jeff Weiss:

> It was one of the most powerful and (gasp) inspiring moments I've ever witnessed in this town. No less than DJ Quik said that it was the biggest public gathering he'd seen since the 1984 Olympics. When the Lakers descended down the purple steps [in the Coliseum], it was the closest any of us will ever know what it was like to watch the Roman Legions returning home after a tour of Gaul.

It was the day Bryant dreamed of all his life, although by the time it arrived—at age 30—he had had so many ups and downs he could hardly believe it. He had done it the hard way, with rare artistry, an iron will, and a dedication never seen before…all of which he had needed to dig himself out of the ruin his career had become.

And he wasn't through. With a deep and young roster and Ron Artest arriving in a deal a few weeks later, anything was possible: more titles, a true Age of Kobe.

Or not. That was the problem with the Lakers. You could never be sure which was coming next, the best or the worst of times.

★ ★ ★

It was the rainbow's end in the NBA. Boston had tradition and New York was New York, but Los Angeles was where all the players wanted to be.

However uncertain the Lakers' legacy had been, they built the franchise on glamour, from the '60s when Wilt Chamberlain made the Philadelphia 76ers trade him there to the '70s when Kareem Abdul-Jabbar arrived from Milwaukee to the '90s when Shaquille O'Neal left Orlando to play in L.A.

*Conquering heroes: The Lakers trot down the Coliseum party steps on a purple carpet.*

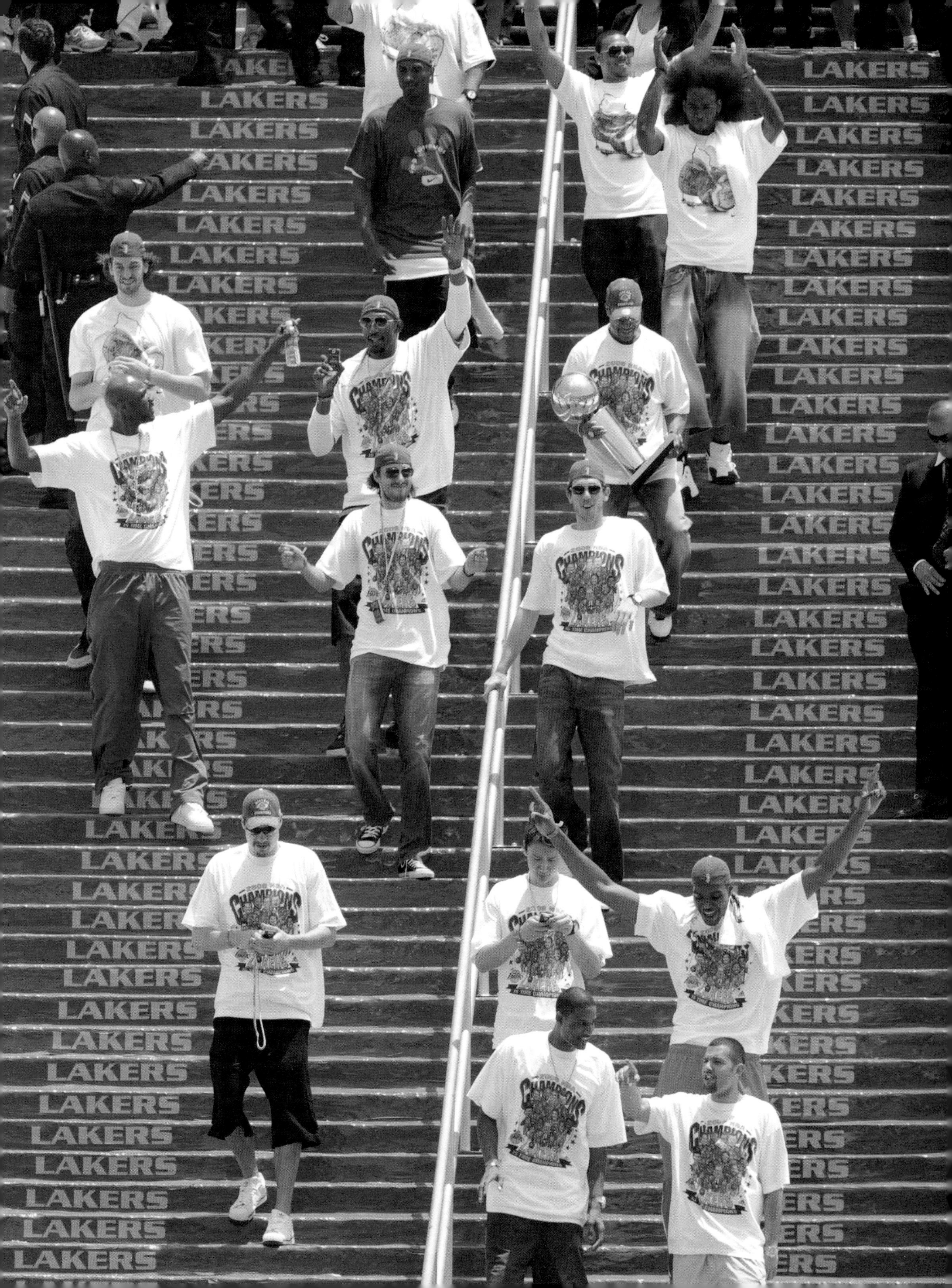
LAKERS
CHAMPIONS

*Giddy Laker fans in old (8) and new (24) Kobe jerseys, Chick Hearn jerseys, and other purple-and-yellow regalia pack the Coliseum.*

The lure of the Golden Land never changed, as Wilt wrote in his 1973 autobiography:

> I grew to love the beauty and informality of Southern California. Everyone there seemed to be "doing his own thing," long before that phrase became fashionable. Girls were prettier and less inhibited and more independent and even the guys seemed more free and open and honest.

In the '80s, when Johnson's "Showtime" Lakers won five titles, the Lakers moved into an ascendancy rarely seen for an NBA team. Even as the once-lordly Dodgers continued to draw 3 million fans annually and won World Championships in 1981 and 1988, and the Raiders won the Super Bowl in 1984, the Lakers still took over the town.

Dodger Stadium, perched above downtown, was a showcase, but for years the Forum, on the flight path to LAX in deteriorating Inglewood, was where the stars went. Coach Pat Riley, who had never acted, was offered the lead for the 1988 movie *Tequila Sunrise* by his friend, director Robert Towne. When Riley said no, Towne made do with Kurt Russell, making him slick his hair back like Riley's. Riley even loaned Russell some clothes.

Riley's friend Michael Douglas also wore his hair like Pat's as Gordon Gekko in *Wall Street*. When Douglas won the Academy Award, Riley wired him, "I have to believe it was all in the hair."

One of the best descriptions of the era came from Cookie Johnson, Magic's girl from back home—whom he married in 1991, late in his career—who wrote this passage for his 1995 autobiography:

> When you're talking about Earvin and women, the first thing you have to understand is L.A. is a big part of the story. If Earvin Johnson had been drafted by Cleveland, Detroit, Milwaukee, or even New York, we would have been married a long time ago. But L.A. is totally different. It's the land of stars, the land of fantasy.
>
> He was only 20 when he moved there and started meeting all those beautiful people. And many of them really are beautiful. In all my life, I've never seen so many stunning women out to catch somebody. The plastic surgery, the gorgeous clothes, you see it all….
>
> The Forum is like Fantasy Land. It's all so out in the open….The first time I went, I watched as a girl in a bright orange dress, tight and low-cut with her boobs hanging out, strolled and strutted all the way around the court. It was incredible. Men actually wrote numbers on pieces of paper and held them up, like judges in the Olympics. She walked over to where Jack Nicholson was sitting. She bent over and said something to him and then walked back to the guy who brought her and gave him a hug. You could never see that anywhere else….
>
> Showtime wasn't just on the court. Part of the show was all those gorgeous women walking around the Forum on

*Finally, a dynasty. Magic Johnson forged a new tradition in the '80s wars with the Celtics and, here, Dennis Johnson.*

*Mr. Laker, Jerry West, beneath his trademark No. 44.*

display. And the players noticed, definitely. They'd be at the free throw line and on the bench and they'd look, too. They'd start thinking, "Well, I guess this is mine for the taking." And they were right.

In 1999, with Showtime long over and Shaq and Kobe trying to carry on the tradition, the Lakers moved downtown to the Staples Center, an arena named for an office supply superstore in which they were only a tenant, but the glitz only got glitzier. In no other dressing room could you have heard a conversation like this in 2000, between player John Salley and radio announcer Paul Sunderland.

Sunderland: "Did you see *The Green Mile*?"
Salley: "I read for it."
Laker Rick Fox read for it, too, but said he was told he was "too pretty," although he went on to have an acting career of his own. They were living legends, assuming one thing: they always had to win.

★ ★ ★

The price the Lakers paid to live this dream—or, at least, those who weren't too tortured to live any dream—was the expectation of constant excellence. When they achieved it, the world was theirs. When they didn't, the world fell in on them.

Great traditions are built by great players who have a spirit that transcends that of other great players and inspires future greats, who become just as driven, or haunted, to match their feats. The Laker tradition in Los Angeles was inseparable from the career of Jerry West, whose silhouette is on the NBA logo but who was totally identified with the franchise he led as player, coach, and GM for most of its first 40 years in town.

Movie-star handsome, well spoken, personable, beloved by peers and fans alike, West was nonetheless the poet laureate of misery. Wearing his torment on his sleeve and making himself all the more endearing, he was in such pain, physically and emotionally, that he seemed to be on the verge of quitting for most of those 40 years.

"I had so many injuries," he once said of his playing career. "I was tired of having needles stuck in me. Tired of having my nose straightened, tired of getting stitches, tired of getting my teeth replaced.

"I took shots because I wanted to play, and players wouldn't do that today, and I know that. And I wouldn't ask one of our players to do it because it's the wrong thing to do….I could sit in the locker room before a game, I could hold my hand out, and sweat would be just dripping off. I don't know if that's the way an athlete's supposed to be, but that's the way I was."

In an era in which the Lakers had a reputation as glamorous losers, West blamed himself for every defeat, up to and including the worst of all, Game 7 of the 1969 Finals, when the Celtics beat them beneath the balloons that grandiose owner Jack Kent Cooke had penned up in the Forum ceiling for the victory celebration.

That was the series in which West became the only member of a losing team to ever be named Finals MVP, and John Havlicek embraced him afterward, telling him, "I love you."

For West, losing was intolerable, and winning was confusing. After the 1985 Finals when he was GM, and they finally beat the Celtics, he didn't go to the games in Boston or attend the parade at home. "If I go to the parade, they'll be cheering me," he told Steve Springer of the *Los Angeles Times*. "I'll be a big hero to them. And then if I make a pick in the draft they don't like, they'll boo me. You know something? I don't need their boos, and I don't need their cheers."

Magic Johnson was capable of enjoying himself in victory, or most other times, but took defeat as hard as West. When Magic's misplays played a large part in their 1984 loss to the Celtics, he went home, locked himself in for days, and wouldn't even talk to his mother on the phone.

Then there was Bryant, a three-time NBA champion and four-time All-Star by age 23, when it all started to go wrong. He was 24 when he was arrested on a rape charge; 25 when his partnership with Shaq ended, precipitating the Lakers' fall into mediocrity; and 28 when he despaired of ever seeing light at the end of the tunnel and lashed out at the organization, accusing owner Jerry Buss of lying to him and demanding to be traded.

It was only two years from Kobe's 2007 days of rage to their parade in 2009, in an adventure beyond anything even they had ever seen.

*The spotlight is on Kobe Bryant, heir apparent to the tradition and the expectations that almost crushed him.*

*That old Lakers tradition: the Celtics' Sam Jones fires away, unobstructed by an unidentified Laker.*

# Bad Times, Good Times

The Celtics were built on decades of greatness. The Lakers were built on decades of choking on the Celtics' dust.

Royalty from a simpler time, the '40s and early '50s, and a simpler place, Minneapolis, the Lakers were strangers in a new land after moving west in 1960. They found themselves becoming golden foils to the game's greatest dynasty, from their first Finals loss to Boston in the '50s, to the six they lost in the '60s. The streak extended into the '80s, when the Celtics made it 8–0.

The Celtics taught the NBA how to play modern basketball, with ensemble casts in which everyone understood his role. The Lakers had superstars, many of whom didn't think in terms of ensembles for their first 20 years in Los Angeles, until Showtime came along in the '80s.

Veterans like Bailey Howell, Paul Silas, and Robert Parish came to Boston to finally win titles. The superstars who launched the Lakers in Southern California spent years in the wilderness trying to win one.

★ ★ ★

The Lakers started, as if in a galaxy far, far away, as rulers of what was then barely even a "bush league," as Wilt Chamberlain would later deride the NBA.

The NBA of the '40s and '50s wasn't even the modern league Wilt sneered at on the cover of *Sports Illustrated* in the mid-1960s. Aside from the Minneapolis Lakers, who were a long way from the West Coast, the Pistons were still in

Fort Wayne, Indiana, carrying the name of the owner's company (Zollner Pistons). The team that would become the Sacramento Kings after tours in Kansas City and Cincinnati, was in Rochester, New York. The team that would become the Philadelphia 76ers was in Syracuse, called the Nationals, or Nats. The team that would become the Washington Wizards was in Chicago, from where it would move to Baltimore.

Nevertheless, the early Lakers had the NBA's very first star, George Mikan, although they didn't make stars then the way they did later. NBA prehistory is often dated back to the night the Lakers arrived at (the old) Madison Square Garden to see the marquee announcing:

WED BASKETBALL
GEO MIKAN VS. KNICKS

Mikan's Lakers won five titles between 1949 and 1954, inspiring the first national interest. The Dumont Network paid the league $39,000 to televise a 13-game package but dropped it after one season.

Mikan was an unlikely matinee idol, with wavy hair, Coke-bottle glasses, and a gentle demeanor, having studied for the priesthood. When he first walked into the Laker dressing room in Sheboygan, Wisconsin, wearing a storm coat and a homburg, the team's star, Jim Pollard, said he was "the biggest-looking dumb character that I'd ever seen for a guy that was barely 23 years old."

At a well-toned 265 pounds, which he threw around enthusiastically, Mikan was no dinosaur. He was more like the first giant NBA

center to walk erect. Dorky as he looked, he also had the first requirement of stardom: he wanted to be a star.

"They had a rookie from Tennessee named Lefty Walther," the late Pete Newell, a former Laker GM, once said. "The kid was a real good player. They're playing a game, and Mikan is in the post, and the guy drives right by Mikan, goes in for a layup. Mikan's got his hand up for the ball, he's the top dog. He gets mad and yells at him.

"The next time the kid gets the ball, he drives, and his man and Mikan's man go up to block the shot. The third time he drives, his guy, Mikan's man, and Mikan all go after the shot.

"Mikan's thing was, 'They're paying you $5,000 to play out there, and they're paying me whatever to play in there, so when I ask for the ball, darn it, give it to me.'

"The kid was gone in a few games."

With Mikan retiring in 1956, the Lakers started to rebuild around *wunderkind*-rookie Elgin Baylor, who led them back to the Finals in 1959, where the Celtics swept them 4–0 in their first Finals meeting. The Lakers were so dependent on Baylor that they moved their training camp to Fort Sam Houston, Texas, before his second season because Elgin had to serve time with his Army Reserve unit and could work out with them only when he was off duty.

It was a tender moment in American race relations, with *Brown v. Topeka Board of Education* only a few years old. Nevertheless, there was no question as to who the Lakers' leader was from the day Baylor arrived.

"Baylor flew in the night before the opening game in Minneapolis," said teammate Rudy

*Elgin Baylor, who might have been the greatest Laker with good knees, slices through the Celtics defense.*

LaRusso, a rookie in Elgin's second season. "He had practiced with us five or six days a month earlier. He suited up and got 52 opening night. I had never seen anything like this in my life....

"It became obvious real quick. Elgin Baylor wasn't black—he was Elgin Baylor. He had the respect and admiration of the veteran players that were on the team at that time. It was clear to me, he was the guy."

That 1959–60 season, their last in Minneapolis, was a 25–50 disaster. Owner Bob Short, who owned a local trucking company, moved them to Los Angeles. With no plans to move himself, Short offered the coaching job to one of his old stars, Vern Mikkelsen. Short even threw in a percentage of the team, although it didn't mean much with half the Minneapolis Chamber of Commerce already owning pieces.

Mikkelsen turned Short down and spent the rest of his life listening to his kids ask what their share would be worth now. "I didn't think he'd get the thing to Sioux Falls [South Dakota], much less to L.A.," said Mikkelsen, "but he did."

★ ★ ★

Los Angeles, once as remote as Hawaii, was going major league in a big way. The Rams, who had come from Cleveland in 1946, fit in perfectly with a high-scoring style, high-profile quarterback controversies, and Hollywood-friendly hunks like Bob Waterfield, who married Jane Russell, and Elroy "Crazylegs" Hirsch, who played himself in the movie *Crazylegs, All American.*

The Dodgers arrived from Brooklyn in 1958 like conquering heroes. Owner Walter O'Malley got lease rights for a new stadium on a hilltop overlooking downtown, which required the removal of the people living there and approval of a hotly contested referendum. The team then rose from seventh place in its first season to win the 1959 World Series before horn-blowing, sun-splashed crowds of 90,000 in the Coliseum.

The Lakers arrived without the negotiations with city officials, the hilltop, the referendum, the wrangling, or any fanfare whatsoever. It was more like Short dropped them off on the doorstep of the new Sports Arena and then went back to the depot in Minneapolis.

The moment—if not the Lakers' arrival—seemed auspicious. The Sports Arena had just opened in 1960 with the Democratic Convention that nominated John F. Kennedy after Eugene McCarthy's rousing speech in favor of Adlai Stevenson. No one even knew the Lakers were coming when the building went up. The prime tenants were USC and UCLA. When there were conflicts, the Lakers went elsewhere, like Cal State–L.A. or the Shrine Auditorium.

"There was really no attention at all," said Jerry West, a rookie that season. "I'll never forget, one night the Laker players went to a Dodger game at the Coliseum. Wally Moon was hitting his home runs over that little short fence in left field. We were there en masse, and they introduced us, and it was like no one even knows who in the heck we are."

Elgin Baylor was in a prime few would see. A 6'5", 225-pound power forward who transcended positions much as Magic Johnson would, bringing the ball up against presses, delighting in challenging Bill Russell himself, freezing him with

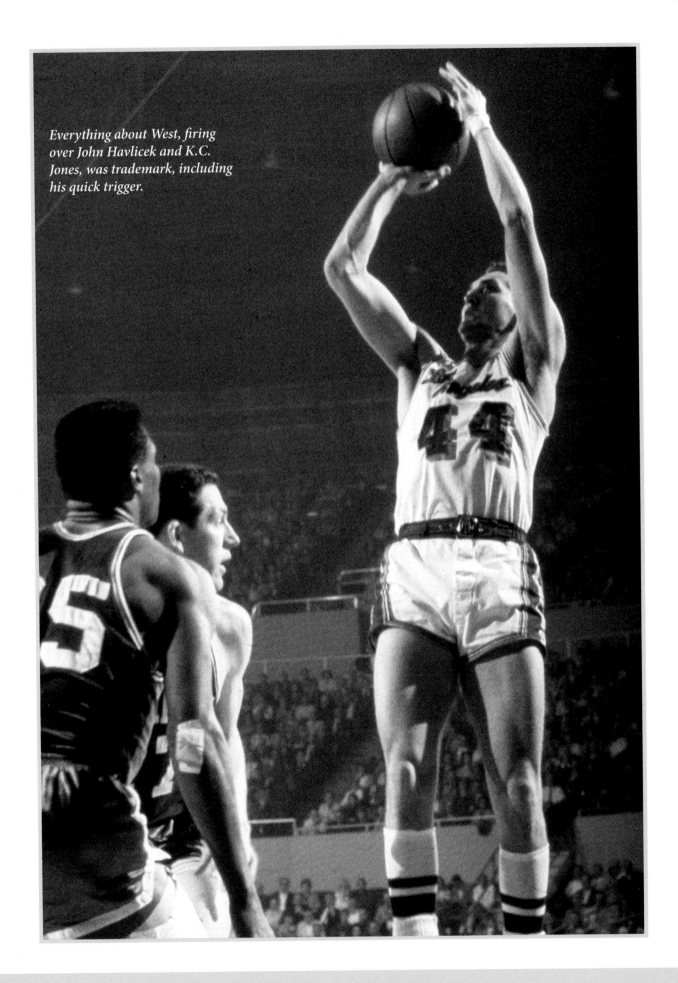

*Everything about West, firing over John Havlicek and K.C. Jones, was trademark, including his quick trigger.*

hesitation moves so that Elgin was said to have discovered how to "hang in the air."

With Jerry West they turned the Lakers into an annual power—in the Western Conference. In their first nine years in town they reached the Finals six times…and lost to Russell and the Celtics each time. The difference was simple. The Celtics had Russell at center. The Lakers had journeymen like Jim Krebs, Leroy Ellis, and Ray Felix, who, after their Game 7 loss to the Celtics in 1962, was supposed to have said, "We'll get them tomorrow."

If they were portrayed as losers, the Lakers were glamorous losers. Jack Nicholson was a young B actor making biker movies when the reigning stars began turning up, with the glamorous Doris Day becoming a courtside regular. Completing the Laker Trinity with Baylor and West, announcer Chick Hearn came aboard when they made the playoffs in their first season (before, there had been no broadcast crew, no radio games, and, of course, no TV). Hearn called the game with as much style as they played it, from his perch "high above the western sideline" where he transported listeners into another world with a language all its own: "Dribble drive!" "Slam dunk!" "He fires from the popcorn machine!" "Heartbrrreak!"

In a market that liked to hear the action narrated, Hearn was all-important. When the Dodgers played the Chicago White Sox in the 1959 World Series, out-of-town writers were amazed to see thousands of fans listening to new transistor radios, so Vin Scully could tell them what they were seeing. The first $1-million-a-year Dodger wouldn't be Sandy Koufax, Don Drysdale, or Steve Garvey, but Vin. Hearn had to make a nightly announcement—which he loved—asking fans to turn their radios down, lest the accumulated volume go over the air as feedback.

The only cloud in the sky seemed to waft in every spring from Boston, with the Celtics beating them in the Finals in 1962, 1963, 1965, 1966, and 1968. Sometimes the Lakers came close, as in 1962, when Frank Selvy missed a 12-footer that would have won Game 7 in regulation, before they lost in overtime. And sometimes they didn't.

In 1968, Jack Kent Cooke acquired Chamberlain, seeming to amass the most powerful basketball team ever with Wilt, West, and Baylor. Instead, it became a year-long power struggle between Chamberlain and coach Butch van Breda Kolff, a tough-talking ex-marine, with so much back and forth that the *Herald-Examiner* became known as "Wilt's paper" and the *Times* as "Butch's paper."

The Lakers went 55–27, a far cry from what was expected, but they still reached the Finals and brought the series back home for Game 7, tied 3–3. There, in Cooke's new Forum, with balloons penned in the ceiling for the postgame celebration, the aging Celtics, who had finished fourth in the East in Russell's last hurrah, beat the Lakers 108–106 in the new low point in Lakers history.

The Lakers, who had trailed by 17, had cut it to eight when Chamberlain the indestructible, who once averaged more than 48 minutes per game, took himself out after hurting his knee. When the Lakers closed in and Wilt got up to return, van Breda Kolff told him to sit back down.

"We weren't as good," West would say of the Celtic wars. "Luck plays such an element in sports, and people don't want to say that. And I'm not saying the Celtics were lucky to beat us because that's not the case…."

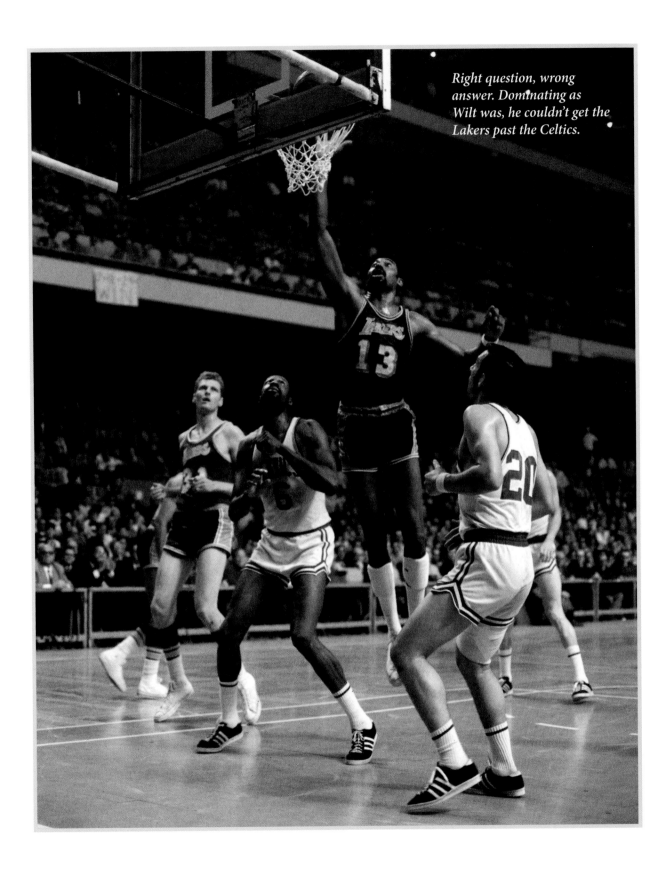

Right question, wrong answer. Dominating as Wilt was, he couldn't get the Lakers past the Celtics.

*Lakers center Wilt Chamberlain vs. future Lakers center Kareem Abdul-Jabbar.*

"It was like a slap in the face. Like, 'We're not gonna let you win, we don't care how well you play.' I always thought it was personal. I got to where I didn't think I was doing enough. I was searching everything that I had ever done in my life for a reason, looking for an answer why.... It almost controlled my life."

★ ★ ★

A year later the Lakers met the Knicks in another classic Finals. That was the one in which Jerry West sent Game 3 into overtime with a shot from behind halfcourt. Willis Reed topped that by dragging his numbed left leg out to start Game 7, as the Knicks blasted the Lakers to win the title. The Lakers weren't merely Celtic foils any more, just foils.

The surprise came two years later when the aging Lakers broke through; a new coach, Bill Sharman, the former Celtic great, persuaded Chamberlain to concentrate on defense as Russell had. They proceeded to win a record 69 games, then stormed through the playoffs with a 12–3 mark.

In a cruel irony, they caught fire when Baylor, who could have been the greatest Laker of them all with good knees, announced his retirement after Sharman told him he would be benched. With second-year forward Jim McMillan taking Elgin's place on November 5, 1971, they started a 33-game winning streak, another record, and never looked back.

A picture captured West and Pat Riley coming off the floor arm-in-arm. Riley looked jubilant, West just intent on getting off the floor.

Riley later wrote of West in his book *Show Time*:

> When we won the championship, he came into the locker room, had a sip of champagne, shook a few hands, and left.

As dominating as the Lakers had been, it wasn't their turn for a Celtic-like run; it was just a moment in time when their stars were all aligned. They weren't the Celtics, who knew how to win. This was Ego City, where Cooke infuriated the players by giving them $1,500 bonuses, $3,500 less than the year before.

The next season, with their veterans another year older, they fell to 60–22 and lost 4–1 to the Knicks in the Finals. The next fall, Chamberlain retired to coach the ABA's San Diego Conquistadors, the last act in his long-running series of contract fights with Cooke. A year later, in the fall of 1975, West, who had mused about retiring almost daily for years, finally did.

"We had just gotten beat by the Milwaukee Bucks," Riley wrote. "Jerry had a muscle tear that would never get better.… Jerry was soaping up in the shower when he turned to me and said, 'This is my last game.'"

The West-Baylor-Chamberlain era was over. The Lakers had had their moments, just not very many.

The three Lakers legends, individually, if not collectively [(l to r) Baylor, Chamberlain, and West].

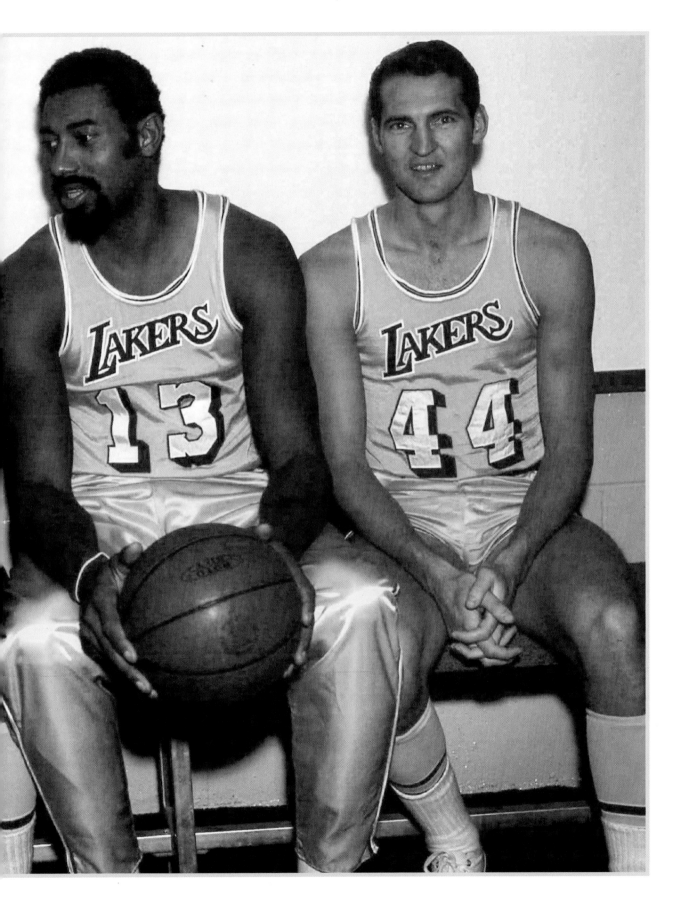

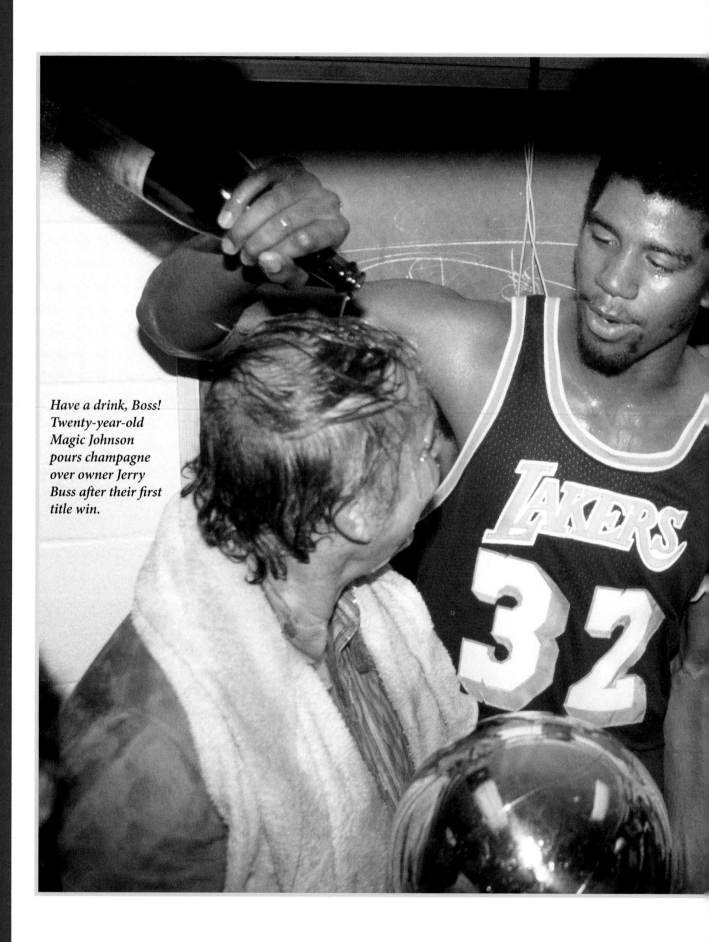

*Have a drink, Boss! Twenty-year-old Magic Johnson pours champagne over owner Jerry Buss after their first title win.*

# At Long Last, Showtime

Then—after all those years when the Lakers were the Washington Generals to whatever team was that season's Harlem Globetrotters—everything changed.

In 1979, owner Jack Kent Cooke, enmeshed in a high-stakes divorce that obliged him to leave the state to avoid being served, sold his "Fabulous Forum," for $67.5 million to Jerry Buss. A former aerospace worker with a PhD in chemistry, Buss had made a fast fortune in the booming Southern California real estate market and was now making up for a hardscrabble youth with a *Playboy* lifestyle like that of his friend Hugh Hefner.

Buss wasn't just smart and daring but lucky, arriving just in time to draft Magic Johnson with a gift No. 1 pick the Lakers had gotten from the New Orleans Jazz three years before for signing free agent Gail Goodrich. The effervescent Johnson, then 20, became the perfect complement to Kareem Abdul-Jabbar in the upcoming decade the NBA was to know as Showtime.

Buss wrote his own rules. He partied with Johnson, and, after winning a title in his first season, gave Magic a "lifetime contract"—$25 million over 25 years—that spread consternation among the other players, starting with veterans like Abdul-Jabbar and Jamaal Wilkes.

Then there was the day in year three (things were happening fast) when Buss fired coach Paul Westhead and tried to give his job to GM Jerry West, who lateraled it to assistant coach Pat Riley, right in front of everybody.

As a coach, Riley, an afterthought as journeyman reserve, color commentator, and fledgling assistant, went on to become as big a star as any of his players, as they won four more titles in the '80s. With five in the decade to Boston's three and victories over the Celtics in 1985 and 1987, the Lakers started a whole new tradition as starry as the heavens.

Buss was that lucky. The '80s were that exciting. The Showtime Lakers were that good.

★ ★ ★

A lot of things came together for the Lakers in the '80s, or a lot of people. As Johnson fit perfectly with Abdul-Jabbar, West, who became GM, was an ideal fit with Buss, who had idolized him as a player and trusted him completely as an administrator.

West had been so miserable after retiring as a player that he returned to coach under Cooke, whom he disliked then, and disliked even more by the time he fled three years later.

"You hear about movie stars who have done it all and just go fruitcake?" West's friend, Gary Colson, then coaching at Pepperdine, asked *Sports Illustrated*'s Rich Hoffer. "I had this fear, you know, a Marilyn Monroe type of thing. What else was there? What would he do now that the cheering had stopped? He was searching for something. It was a depression that all great actors and athletes go through."

Almost heaven: Chick Hearn, high above the western sideline of the Forum, as he used to put it, with color man Lynn Schackleford.

*Pat Riley, who went from their little buddy to their taskmaster, at work in Boston Garden.*

Johnson's impact was dramatic. Coming off the most-watched basketball game ever, Michigan State's victory over Larry Bird's Indiana State in the NCAA Finals, he jumped into Abdul-Jabbar's arms in his NBA debut, after Kareem hit a game-winning shot in San Diego, startling the veteran who rarely showed any emotion, much less joy.

"We're in our first game, and Kareem hits that sky hook down in San Diego, and Magic is wrapped around his neck," said Michael Cooper, a second-year player that season. "He's jumping up and down like we've just won a championship…. Kareem says, 'Hey, what you doing, guy? We still got 81 more games to play.'"

All the Lakers veterans rolled their eyes at Johnson's assumption that his arrival had changed everything. In training camp, where Magic played as if he were in the Finals, Norm Nixon named him "Buck," short for "Young Buck." It became Johnson's favorite nickname, which only teammates could call him.

The joke was on the veterans. The season ended with Kareem out and Johnson jumping center in Game 6 of the Finals, scoring 42 points with 15 rebounds and seven assists in a 123–107 upset of the 76ers. Said Buss, hugging the Walter A. Brown Trophy and wiping champagne out of his eyes, "You don't know how long I've waited for this."

Who needed perspective if they were that good? If no one had realized how great Johnson was before, they did now. He wasn't called Magic because he did card tricks.

★ ★ ★

One more major move would be needed to reconfigure the Lakers, and it was at hand, after the dancing stopped in Johnson's second season.

*In the beginning, there were no smiles between Magic Johnson and Larry Bird. As their friendship grew, they were just as determined to beat the other.*

Magic missed 45 games with a knee injury. Teammates, who'd had it up to here with Buss' favoritism, were further irritated to see the team hand out "The Magic is Back" buttons when he returned. On the eve of the playoffs Nixon sneered at Magic in the press, in a major rift between the close friends. They then were stunned in the first round by Houston, 2–1, with Magic breaking off a play for Kareem at the end of Game 3 to shoot a runner that missed everything.

A year later, the players all but mutinied against coach Paul Westhead. Johnson announced he wanted to be traded, ending Westhead's tenure, prompting the craziest press conference in NBA history, as Buss tried to finesse West into taking over by naming him "offensive coach," with assistant Pat Riley as "co-coach."

West was stunned. The press wasn't sure what it was hearing.

Buss [taking a drag on his cigarette]: I did not specifically make someone head coach and someone else assistant coach. That was not accidental. I did it the way I announced on purpose. I feel that Pat is very capable of running the Laker team. However, I feel that we need a new offensive coach. I asked Jerry if he'd take the job, and fortunately, because of his relationship with Pat, I feel the two of them will coach this team together, with Jerry being in charge of the offense in particular. Q: There will be a game tomorrow night. The game will end. Will two coaches come out and talk to us? Or will they choose which one it's going to be from game to game?

*The Celtics played rough. Here Scott Wedman pounces on Byron Scott, literally.*

Buss [grinning]: We discussed that. In that I'm really making this change to change the offense, and since Jerry West will be in charge of the offense, he will be the one you will question. [Smiling] You can, however, talk to Pat whenever you want, as well.

Q: Who picks the starting lineup?

Buss [grinning uneasily]: Oh, which one of these two? Uh, I think there are some things along the line, not only the starting lineups but other considerations as well—uh, potential trades, etcetera, etcetera—that Pat and Jerry are going to have to sit down and work out what their responsibilities are.

West [invited by Buss to clear up the confusion]: First of all, I want to clear up one thing. I'm going to be working for Pat Riley.

Mercifully for the Lakers, the story remained Johnson's effrontery, as Laker fans trashed Magic in letters to the editor ("It has taken him only two seasons to go from Magic to Tragic"..."His next contract should be with Gerber's baby food"). The farcical announcement of the new coach got little attention. As Riley joked, "If no one else wants it, I'll take it."

With Riley giving the players their head, or letting the players do anything they wanted, they won 21 of his first 27 games, finished No. 1 in the West, went on to the Finals, and beat the 76ers 4–2.

One thing remained, a certain curse. In 1984, the Lakers and Celtics met in the Finals for the first time since the balloon game in 1969, and the first with Johnson and Bird renewing their college rivalry. The Lakers looked stronger, leading in the last minute of Games 1–4. The Celtics stole two of them back, starting when Gerald Henderson intercepted James Worthy's pass in the backcourt at the end of regulation in Game 2 and laid it in to force an overtime, which Boston won.

The ground rules changed in Game 4, when Kevin McHale clotheslined Kurt Rambis. Riley decided their manhood was at stake and told his players to fight back, but they couldn't wrestle and run at the same time. The Celtics went up 3–2 by winning Game 5 on a hot Friday night that turned Boston Garden into a steam bath and finished the Lakers off back there in Game 7.

The Lakers huddled overnight in their downtown hotel as Celtic fans bayed into the early hours of the morning. Johnson stayed up with his friends, Isiah Thomas and Mark Aguirre. Riley, who stayed up all night with assistant coach Bill Bertka and their wives, called it "the longest night of my life."

"The whole series was a disaster for me," Johnson said. "I let the clock run down in Game 2. We go back there for Game 7, another crucial play, I had James open, I could have gotten it to him, and DJ [Dennis Johnson] took it from me.

"It hurt so bad. We hurt. All of us hurt. It was just heartbreaking. Riles was like a crazy man. But when we got out of there, we learned a valuable lesson. Only the strong survive, and that's something we didn't know until then. Talent just don't get it. We realized it's not all about talent, and that's the first time the Lakers ever encountered that, someone who was stronger minded.

"So we said, 'Okay, we got to be stronger.'"

The next season was a campaign to return to the Finals, hoping for a rematch. It happened, too—whereupon the Celtics destroyed them 148–114 in Game 1 in Boston, known thereafter as the Memorial Day Massacre.

Lakers history pivoted on the two days before Game 2, when a furious Riley, no longer their little bobo, visited a cold rage on his players, starting with an incendiary film review in which he railed at Kareem, who had been embarrassed by Robert Parish beating him down the floor. Then came two days of practice when Riley wouldn't even talk to them.

"He was so mad, I mean, I was scared to talk to him, and I usually talk to him," Johnson said. "I tell you what, it was the greatest coaching strategy that I've ever seen, because when we came out the next night, we were ready. Kareem was ready. You know what I'm saying?"

Abdul-Jabbar went for 30 points, 17 rebounds, eight assists, and three blocks in Game 2. The Lakers led by 18 at the half and won 109–102.

The Lakers won in six games, stomping the Celtics 110–100 in Game 6 in Boston Garden. Celtic fans streamed out early, like the Lakers fans they had sneered at.

Proving the curse was over, the Lakers beat Boston again in 1987, in a series in which the aging Celtics did well to last six games.

A year later, the Lakers became the first team to repeat in 19 years, beating Detroit's Bad Boy Pistons in a tough seven-game series. With five titles in the '80s to the Celtics' three, the Lakers were a grown-up power, at last.

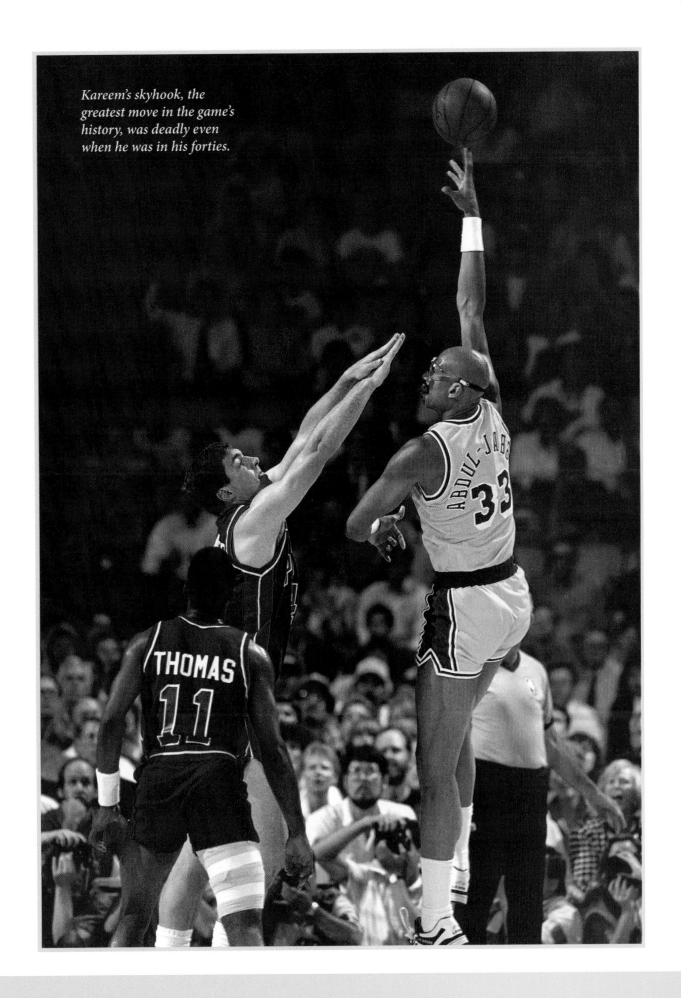

*Kareem's skyhook, the greatest move in the game's history, was deadly even when he was in his forties.*

The greatest two-man tandem in the game's history—when they felt like it.

# Shaq and Kobe

Showtime didn't end in a thunderclap, it just seemed that way in the fall of 1991, when Magic Johnson retired in a press conference shown around the world, having just learned he was HIV-positive.

As far as dominating anyone, that had already ended when Kareem Abdul-Jabbar retired two years before. Without Kareen the following season, Pat Riley, now a full-grown taskmaster, and Johnson, anxious to win a title without Kareem, had lashed the team to a No. 1 finish in the West, but they had then been stunned in the second round by Phoenix.

With players grumbling about the lash, Riley was eased out the door. The Lakers paid a courtesy call to the Finals in 1991 under rookie coach Mike Dunleavy but fell to Michael Jordan's Bulls 4–1.

*17-year-old Kobe Bryant joins the Lakers in 1996.*

Magic's dramatic announcement came the next fall. That ended that.

It began a bleak period, with the Lakers falling into the lottery for the first time. Of course, it lasted only five years, from Johnson's press conference in 1991 to the one before the Olympics began in Atlanta in 1996, announcing the signing of Shaquille O'Neal.

In Jerry West's masterpiece as GM, they landed O'Neal and 17-year-old Kobe Bryant within seven days. On July 11, they completed a deal with Charlotte, trading center Vlade Divac for the rights to Bryant. On July 18 they used the money they had freed up to sign O'Neal.

Only a few insiders grasped the significance of what had just happened. One was Danny Ainge, then coach of the Phoenix Suns, who had tried to trade up for Bryant on draft day too, only to be turned down by Golden State, which had No. 11 but used it for North Carolina State's Todd Fuller.

When Charlotte then took Bryant at No. 13 for delivery to the Lakers, amid mounting speculation they would land O'Neal, Ainge says he exclaimed to no one in particular, "Oh my gosh, they've got Shaq and Kobe."

That would have been the first time anyone said the words "Shaq and Kobe." Tens of thousands more mentions awaited.

★ ★ ★

As a couple, they were so unlikely that there was no thought that they were a couple at all. O'Neal was a 7'1", 325-pound savior, sent to restore the Lakers to greatness. Bryant was a skinny high

school kid from Lower Merion, Pennsylvania, on the tony Main Line, who had caught West's eye but could hardly be expected to play a major role for years.

Actually, Kobe was to prospects what Shaq was to big men, a once-in-a-generation player. Bryant had caught more eyes than West's, including those of Ainge and Clipper coach Bill Fitch. Incredibly, Ainge and Fitch had both said the same thing West had: Bryant's workout for them was the best they'd ever seen.

O'Neal, who habitually befriended young guys, tried to take Bryant under his wing in their first training camp. Kobe delicately removed Shaq's wing from his shoulder. After that, Shaq began calling him "Showboat," in a preview of what lay ahead.

There was no holding the Golden Child back. With West and Buss head over heels for Bryant, coach Del Harris tried to win Kobe over, letting him take the final shot in their final game of the season, a Game 5 defeat at Utah in the second round. Kobe wound up taking four key shots in regulation and overtime—and airballed all four.

By their third season, when Kobe became a starter, Shaq was dropping hints about his displeasure. By their fourth, when coach Phil Jackson arrived, since Shaq and Kobe had yet to win a title, their rift surfaced.

By their fifth season, coming off the 2000 title that surprised Jackson as much as anyone, the rift became a feud. Kobe said he might have to go elsewhere to be all he could, Shaq said that was fine, and Phil said he'd help Kobe leave, if that was what he wanted. Remarkably, after all that, they pulled it together at season's end to win their last

*The road to the title goes through here: the Lakers won in 2000, 2001, and 2002, though failing to win their conference twice and their division once.*

eight games, then blitzed through the playoffs with a 15–1 record and won their second title.

This wasn't an ordinary feud. They weren't ordinary combatants. Ainge said it was like seeing what would have happened if Michael Jordan had ever played with Wilt Chamberlain.

Bryant's frustration was understandable, convinced as he was that he had a destiny to be the best ever, which he said he realized at age six. He wasn't exactly selfish, as people who saw him launch shots thought, but he was self-obsessed.

The darling of his family, the youngest son after two daughters, he set out to follow his father, Joe, a former NBA player, whom he idolized.

They could have been the Cosbys, with the kids all well-spoken, polite, dutiful, getting good grades, and excelling at whatever sports they played. As far as basketball went, however, Kobe might have been raised by wolves, in his single-minded pursuit of his destiny. His physical talent was eye-popping, but it was his skill level that separated him from other phenoms. The last prospect like him had been Michael Jordan, and not even Mike had been that advanced at 17. The next would be LeBron James, seven years later.

The game was easy for Kobe. Things like growing up and superstardom were hard. His feud with O'Neal in the 2000–01 season hid a more tragic rift with his parents about his plans to marry Vanessa Laine, a 17-year-old high school senior. The fight grew so bitter that Joe and Pam Bryant moved back to Philadelphia.

Shaq and Kobe were fine for two seasons after that, when the issue became O'Neal's conditioning, with Shaq coming in ever heavier, getting hurt more often, and taking longer to play himself into shape. Not that it was impossible, as they proved in the 2001–02 season, winning their third title in a row, sweeping the Nets in the Finals, as Shaq won his third Finals MVP.

A year later, however, they finished No. 5, putting them on the road through the postseason. That was only two rounds, when San Antonio knocked them off, ending their run at three titles.

The real problem in the spring of 2003 came a few weeks later. Bryant, in Colorado for a knee operation the Lakers didn't even know about, was arrested and charged with rape, ending life as he and the Lakers had known it.

★ ★ ★

Determined to lead his life as he always had, Bryant decided to play the 2003–04 season while standing trial. He did everything as before, making himself available to the press before and after games. Now the press included national news magazines, like *Newsweek*, whose Allison Samuels wrote a tough cover piece and was then denied press credentials, not to mention the national tabloids, which offered townspeople in Eagle, Colorado, thousands of dollars for inside info.

Bryant's resolve was steely as ever, but his trademark poise was gone. He was infuriated at O'Neal, who had called and had left a message of support over the summer but gone no further, informing Jackson he would no longer take any bleep off Shaq.

O'Neal knew something Bryant didn't know he knew: Kobe had brought his name into it, telling the officers who arrested him Shaq had paid $1 million to women to make complaints like this go

*Thunderbolt: at a press conference accompanied by his wife, Vanessa, Kobe Bryant acknowledges a sexual encounter but denies assaulting a young woman in Colorado.*

*Nowhere to run: under scrutiny with every step he takes, Bryant walks through the Staples Center with the chief of his security detail, Robert Lara.*

away. Unknown to Bryant, the police had secretly taped him, then called O'Neal, asking to talk to him.

O'Neal declined and didn't say a word about it until the story leaked a year later. Nevertheless, it was clear Shaq had as little use for Kobe as Kobe had for Shaq.

The Lakers had just signed Karl Malone and Gary Payton, who took huge pay cuts. They now fielded one of the greatest lineups ever, but basketball was almost beside the point. On media day, the Lakers set up a cordon around their practice facility, barring any media, credentialed or not, if they looked more interested in the court case than the Lakers' season. Jackson was as calm as ever. Everyone else in the organization was musing about a career change.

"Just assume this is the season from hell, and anything that doesn't go wrong is a bonus," a friend told publicist John Black.

"I just didn't know the flames would be so hot," said Black.

Bryant was out of shape after his knee surgery, so shaken he hadn't worked out all summer. Downcast and beyond being able to hide it— "Every day is a bad day," he said—he went into launch mode in exhibitions, trying to catch up. With O'Neal bristling, Jackson threw out the possibility of "an implosion" in Las Vegas before the last exhibition. Bryant went 3–10 in that one, and O'Neal suggested in the press that he pass more while getting in shape.

"I know how to play my guard spot," Bryant answered in the press. "He can worry about the low post. I'll worry about mine."

Replied O'Neal: "Just ask Karl and Gary why they came here. One person. Not two. One. Period."

Karl and Gary just wanted it to end so they could play ball, which Shaq, at least, promised to do. "It's not going to continue," said Malone at the next practice. "Trust me."

Jackson sent Kobe and Shaq home from practice that day after consulting a professional arbitrator, who suggested separating them to give them a chance to cool down. Kobe proceeded to call ESPN's Jim Gray, a longtime confidant, and dump all over O'Neal, then told Gray to relay what he had said on the air.

Said Bryant through Gray: "There's more to life than whose team this is, but this is his team so it's time for him to act like it. That means no more coming into camp fat and out of shape when your team is relying on your leadership on and off the court. It also means no more blaming others for our team's failure or blaming staff members for not overdramatizing your injuries, so that you avoid blame for your lack of conditioning. Also, 'my team' doesn't mean only when we win. It means carrying the burden of defeat just as gracefully as you carry a championship trophy.

"I don't need Shaq's advice on how to play hurt. I've played with IVs before…with a broken hand, a sprained ankle, a fractured tooth, a severed lip, and a knee the size of a softball. I didn't miss 15 games because of a toe injury that everybody knows wasn't that serious in the first place....

"He is not my quote-unquote 'big brother.' A big brother would have called me up over the summer."

On that note, the Lakers started the 2003–04 season.

* * *

On top of everything else, Bryant was approaching free agency and vowing to sign with the Clippers, who had a promising young roster led by Elton Brand and Corey Maggette. In the exhibition opener at Anaheim, Clipper coach Mike Dunleavy said he was invited to meet secretly with Kobe—which would have been tampering times a thousand—and turned it down, but that Kobe then told him during the game to bring him over. Kobe's agent, Rob Pelinka, also told a Clipper official, "Save your cap room." The Clippers did, from that moment.

Bryant's anger spilled over onto Jackson, who was tacitly allied with Shaq. By January, Jackson, whose contract was running out too, had given up trying to reach Kobe, telling GM Mitch Kupchak he wouldn't be back if they didn't trade Bryant.

It wasn't much of a choice for Buss, who took the exciting 25-year-old demon worker Bryant over the package deal of the 31-year-old, oft-injured, ever-heavier O'Neal (who wanted a three-year, $80 million extension), and the $6 million-per-year Jackson.

With Bryant hurt and the team on the East Coast, Buss met with Kobe on Super Bowl Sunday, February 1, 2004, in the Four Seasons in Newport Beach. While the New England Patriots beat the Carolina Panthers and Janet Jackson had her "wardrobe malfunction," Buss informed Bryant that he wouldn't bring Jackson or O'Neal back. Buss then had the team announce that it had withdrawn its last offer to Jackson and had ended negotiations, making Phil an official lame duck.

It was a crisis a week. Late in the season, the Lakers no-showed in a rout in Sacramento. Bryant took only one shot in the first half as the Kings went up by 19, because he was being double-teamed coming off screens, he said. Of course,

*No longer bulletproof, Bryant's relationship with coach Phil Jackson fell apart.*

*Trying to put Humpty Dumpty together again: the Lakers beat Houston in the first round in 2004.*

his shot totals in the last three games had been 26, 23, and 23, amid the usual muttering, so Kobe could have been giving the ball up to show them what happened when he did. *Los Angeles Times* columnist Bill Plaschke wrote that he had "tanked." A Laker player who didn't want to be identified—but was not O'Neal—told Tim Brown of the *Times*, "I don't know how we can forgive him."

Enraged, Bryant stormed into the practice facility, and with f-bombs flying, demanded to know who had said it. All denied it just as heatedly. As a team official put it that day, "Kobe's melting down."

Bryant went into the stratosphere on the court, too. In the finale at Portland, he hit a leaning three-pointer under Ruben Patterson's armpit to tie it at the end of regulation and a high, arching three over fast-closing Theo Ratliff at the end of the second overtime to win it.

Thus, they embarked on what looked like their last postseason together, where, amazingly, they picked up the pieces and reassembled the franchise, eliminating Houston in the first round. Then with their season passing before their eyes after San Antonio went up 2–0, the Lakers summoned everything they had to come back and beat the Spurs 4–2 in the series.

In Game 4, when the Lakers tied it at two games apiece, Bryant scored 42 points after a dramatic entrance minutes before the tipoff, after flying in from a court appearance in Colorado. Said O'Neal afterward, "Once again, I have to title him as the best player ever."

What about Michael Jordan, someone asked. "What about him?" replied O'Neal.

The Lakers then won the pivotal Game 5 in San Antonio on Derek Fisher's miracle 18-foot hook as time expired, after Tim Duncan's dramatic 22-footer fell with :00.4 left had seemed to win it for the Spurs. Bryant, who had gone back to Colorado on the off-days before rejoining the team, played 47 minutes and needed IV fluids afterward.

The Lakers polished off Minnesota in the Western Conference Finals and advanced to the Finals, where they were expected to make short work of the upstart Detroit Pistons. Everyone seemed about to fall in everyone else's arms yet again. Rick Fox said O'Neal told him, "We need to keep this together, because when it's gone, it's going to be gone." Bryant told a confidant he didn't know if he would opt out after all.

The energetic young Pistons, on a roll under first-year coach Larry Brown, then shocked the world—and ended the Lakers' world—ousting them in five games, winning Games 3, 4, and 5 in Auburn Hills in an ever more thunderous fashion.

Within days, the Lakers had agreed to trade O'Neal to Miami. Derek Fisher left as a free agent that summer. Payton was traded to Boston, along with Fox, who retired. Bryant opted out after all, then went to the 11th hour and 59th minute before deciding to stay.

The Lakers got Kobe new teammates Lamar Odom, Caron Butler, Chris Mihm, and James Jones, so Kobe wasn't facing their brave new world all alone. It was close enough.

*They're baaaaaack? Kobe, always a Spurs killer, pulls the Lakers through in the second round of the playoffs in 2004.*

*Trying to carry the franchise alone, Bryant bristles at everyone around him, including Golden State's Baron Davis.*

# 5

# Outcast

"In about a year or two he'll be calling out to Jerry Buss that 'we need some help in here,' or 'trade me.' And we'll all be saying, 'I told you so.'"

—Ray Allen, fall 2004

"I have been an outcast my entire life."

—Kobe Bryant, *Dime*, January 2006

Then, as the Bill Murray character in *Stripes* says when his girlfriend walks out the door, depression set in.

From owner Jerry Buss down, the Lakers didn't realize that trading Shaquille O'Neal meant they had gone out of the business of being the Lakers. Forget titles. As the 2004–2005 season showed, they weren't even a playoff team.

Bryant's legal peril ended when the young woman decided not to testify, and the prosecution dropped the case, but his personal trials continued. Coach Phil Jackson wrote a tell-all book, *The Last Season*, in which he called

Bryant "uncoachable." The Eagle police's secret tape of Bryant's interrogation was leaked, with Kobe claiming O'Neal had paid $1 million to handle "situations like this."

Sneered Shaq in reply, "I'm not the one paying for love." In a league in which everyone thought of himself as *Scarface*'s Tony Montana (O'Neal's particular favorite), laughing in the cops' faces, Bryant was beneath contempt. It was *Mission: Impossible*, but Bryant wasn't Ethan Hunt. For the first time in his career, as Kobe was about to learn to his dismay, he had no control over his fate.

With only a dim awareness of anyone else's sensitivities, Bryant was astonished by the popular reaction to the breakup. He hadn't wanted to get away from Shaq any more than Shaq wanted to get away from him—and Kobe had assumed all along that he'd be the one to leave. Buss made his decision without Bryant's input, informing him that O'Neal and Jackson wouldn't be back. Kobe had thought he would become a Clipper up until the last moment, and he couldn't understand why no one understood that.

Meanwhile, Shaq was already back in contention, joining young Dwyane Wade in Miami, and zinging Bryant in every other sentence. The Lakers were young wannabes, a reality Bryant had acknowledged when he re-signed. "It's not even close," he said. "We know that. Everybody knows that. We don't have the most dominant player in the game so that's going to change this drastically."

With all the scorn that had been heaped on him since then, Bryant was frantic by the exhibition opener, when he pounced on Seattle's Ray Allen, pressing him all over while scoring 15 of the Lakers' first 20 points. It wasn't personal to Bryant, who hugged Allen afterward, but Allen, who didn't like being called out in the exhibition opener, ripped Bryant publicly for breaking up their team.

Laker hopes rode on their new tandem, but the 6'10" Lamar Odom's talent and versatility were offset by his Ferdinand-the-Bull passivity. Finding himself marooned in mediocrity, a new edgy, defensive Bryant emerged, given to glaring at referees so darkly it looked as if he might melt one. He had already had it with the press in the good times; now it was a constant reminder of his plight. Having accurately described the team's limits in July, a defiant Bryant now told a team official, "What are they going to say when I win five titles with this team?"

It was a disaster from the start. Karl Malone, Bryant's friend and neighbor in Newport Beach, who had been planning to come back to the team, called it off after a dispute in which Vanessa Bryant claimed he had come on to her at a game. Showing how little the organization thought of the Bryants' indignation, Buss and GM Mitch Kupchak had lunch with Malone to make a last-ditch plea for Karl to return. Buss even suggested Karl could work in the front office after his playing career.

Completing the nightmare, Jackson's successor, Rudy Tomjanovich, who was getting $30 million over five years—as much as Buss had paid Phil— fled at midseason, overwhelmed enough to leave $27 million on the table. A recovering alcoholic, Rudy T. found himself taking medication to deal with the stress, which came with the outsized expectations for his team. "This isn't Houston,

*Lamar Odom, who was supposed to be Scottie Pippen to Kobe's Michael Jordan.*

where Rudy was the fair-haired boy," said an old friend. "He was overwhelmed, and he said, 'Who needs it?'"

The Lakers cratered, losing 19 of their last 21. When new point guard Chucky Atkins was asked what they needed, he hissed, "Ask the GM." He didn't mean Kupchak.

Buss held a rare postseason press conference to reassure Laker fans, attributing their fall to Tomjanovich's departure ("a terrible blow") and injuries to worn-out acquisitions such as Vlade Divac and Brian Grant and role players such as Devean George ("I don't know how many teams have ever lost 60 percent of their lineup"), musing about being back in the Western Conference Finals "in a couple of seasons." Meanwhile, Kupchak, asked to address a first-ever "town meeting" of season-ticket holders—whose rate of renewal was alarmingly slow—was asked to resign by one of them.

★ ★ ★

Actually, Tomjanovich had done the Lakers a favor. Now they could go out and get...Phil Jackson?

It wasn't surprising that Jackson's name was on the lips of Lakers fans. It was surprising that he was not only open to returning but, with a range of options that included the Cavaliers and young LeBron James, actually *wanted* to coach the Lakers. Jackson had a pronounced comfort level with people and places he knew. After five years with the Lakers, living on the beach at Playa del Rey and maintaining his relationship with Jeannie Buss, he couldn't have been more comfortable.

Jeannie's dad, who had shown Jackson the door only a year before, looked everywhere else, offering the job to University of Kansas coach Roy Williams. Finally, bowing to the will of the fans, who might otherwise have burned down Staples Center, Buss brought Jackson

*Only you, Phil Jackson. Who else would return to a team that showed him the door and a superstar who hated him?*

*Meanwhile, in Miami, Shaq wins his fourth title in 2006, with young Dwyane Wade in the Kobe role.*

back—at Phil's astronomical price, $33 million for three years.

Asked to comment, Bryant said stonily that Jackson was a "proven winner," and his hiring was "something I support." A year before, all the Lakers had cared about was how Kobe felt; this time they didn't even ask him.

Nevertheless, with one corner of their old triangle gone, it took only a few weeks for Bryant and Jackson to forge a new alliance. If the old one had been like James Dean and his father, played by Jim Backus, in *Rebel Without a Cause*, this was more like Don Vito and Michael Corleone.

Unfortunately, the team was still what it was. Jackson thought Bryant and Odom could be like Michael Jordan and Scottie Pippen, but Lamar wouldn't even average 15 points that season, while taking a career-low 11.6 shots a game. As Jackson's blunt-spoken assistant, Tex Winter, put it, "Scottie's one of the quickest learners I've ever coached. Big difference."

So Jackson turned to Bryant, who cut it loose as never before.

Bryant was now officially an outcast, with Nike, his lone remaining big-ticket sponsor, trading on his fall in a campaign with black-and-white print ads of a somber-looking Kobe, looking like someone in a wanted circular at the post office.

Down the left side of the two-page layout was a vertical list of indictments, alternating with the drills Bryant would do on a day in the off-season.

Ball hog.
*100m run x 10.*
You're garbage.
*100 made free throws.*
Prima donna.
*Lat pulldowns 10 x 4.*
Mental.
*Leg curls 10 x 3.*
Not a team player.
*Film review.*

It wasn't just an advertising pose. The prodigy—who had won three titles by 23 and thought that was how it would always be—suddenly realized he might never win another.

Disinclined as Bryant had always been to acknowledge doubts, he put it all out there in a little-noted, first-person piece for *Dime* magazine, going as far as to question the mission he had devoted his life to.

Am I supposed to obsess myself with winning, only to win, retire, and wonder if all my sacrifices were worth it? Is it okay for me to sacrifice time away from my children, time watching them grow up, missing Easter, Christmas, and other special events, to win a ring?

It was revelation after revelation, stark admissions of feelings he had often displayed but had never acknowledged: anger, fear, disillusionment, alienation…and loneliness.

My biggest fear is not winning another title….I am determined to lead this organization back to the top. The people who once celebrated me are the same people who doubt me now. They say I don't have Shaq, that I can't win, that it's over.…

I remember when I was 15 years old and wanted to be famous and be on TV. That desire didn't motivate me to play or overshadow the essence of the game, but, like any kid, I thought being a celebrity would be cool. As I've gotten older and actually became famous, I realize that it's not what I thought it would be....

I have been an outcast my entire life. From being the only black kid in a town in Italy all the way to when I was 17 and playing in the NBA. What separated me from others more consistently than skin color or age was my hunger. My mission.

I've always been made to feel there was something wrong with wanting to win so badly and wanting to become the best at what you do....I have faced so much criticism for my drive that at times it has alienated me from the majority, the people who are comfortable with second place, the people who hate me because I am not. You know these kind of people; they are the ones who fear winning, the jealous ones who envy and try to sabotage. They are the people who have been telling me I can't win all my life.

Many times my drive to succeed has put me on an island all by myself because no one understood me.

★ ★ ★

As no one else with so much going for him could have gotten into as much trouble, no one in a hole like the one he was in could have dreamed of getting himself out of it, as Bryant would.

Michael Jordan had been the most skilled great athlete anyone had seen. Bryant was wilder than Jordan, a crucial difference, but he was as great an athlete, a better ball handler and shooter, and had a dedication never before seen in one so gifted. If Michael played at a higher level consistently, not even he could match Kobe's peaks.

Now Jackson unleashed Bryant on the world. The first fireworks show came when Kobe got 62 points—in three quarters—before sitting out the fourth in a win over the Mavericks. The buzzing had barely died down when Bryant went for 81, the second-biggest game to Wilt Chamberlain's 100, in a win over Toronto. It wasn't a stunt or a total Kobe got by piling up points in garbage time. The Lakers were 18 points behind early in the third quarter before Bryant, who had 29 to that point, got 51 more in the last 21 minutes.

The reaction around the league, among peers who had long regarded him skeptically, was awe.

"I was actually calling people up on the phone to make sure they were watching it," said then-76er Allen Iverson, "'cause I watched the game from beginning to end."

"I think everybody called every player in the league," said Dwyane Wade. "Maybe I'll go home and play my video game, and maybe I'll get 80."

"Imagine what would have happened if our game had been close," said Dallas' Darrell Armstrong.

Toronto's Jalen Rose, a reserve who reckoned he had given up 20 of Bryant's points, emailed the *New York Post*'s Peter Vecsey. "His expression never changed. And he hit some AMAZING shots...contested LONG 3s...double pump-fake jumpers....I've never seen anything like it...from ANYONE! It

Kobe 62, world 0.
With double-teams a
way of life, Bryant still
gets 62 points in three
quarters against the
Mavericks.

*Andrew Bynum, who joined the Lakers at 17, happens—but not fast enough for Kobe.*

was like playing *NBA Live* but on the arcade level…just…BANANAS….WOW!!!"

Bryant averaged 43 points that January, the highest-scoring month of his career. With his teammates picking it up, they won 11 of their last 14 to finish 45–37, No. 7 in the West, returned to the playoffs, and shocked the No. 2-seeded Suns, going up 3–1, before it all came undone.

The Suns rallied to win 4–3, routing the Lakers 121–90 in Game 7 in Phoenix. As if outlining Bryant's predicament, the sky fell in on him. Noting he had taken only two shots in the second half of Game 7, T.J. Simers of the *Los Angeles Times* wrote that he "tanked." TNT's Charles Barkley called Kobe "selfish" and said he got 20 angry text messages from him.

Petulance wasn't unheard of in great stars. Jordan once took eight shots in a loss in the 1989 Eastern Conference Finals after coach Doug Collins told him to involve teammates. This time, however, Bryant had scored 23 points in the first half, the Suns still led by 15, and Jackson told him not to try to do it on his own. "Kobe went out with the game plan in mind," said Jackson.

Bryant's brilliance of January was as nothing, eclipsed by the team's fall, even if no one had expected the Lakers to do anything. Bryant had definitely chosen the wrong L.A. team. The Clippers, who had finished two games ahead of them at 47–35, went on to reach the second round, getting higher TV ratings locally than the Lakers had. Even Jack Nicholson went to see the Clippers.

Nor were the Clippers shy about letting the Lakers know they were yesterday's news. As Brand said after beating them during the season, "We were better than them last year. We have to shoot for the teams above us."

In the really bad news for the Lakers, they were on a three-year descent to hell, and this was only year two.

★ ★ ★

The 2006–07 season started with Bryant missing the entire preseason after arthroscopic knee surgery. Jackson sat it out, too, after back surgery. The best Kobe came up with on media day was, "Sometimes less is more."

The former Golden Child now embraced a new nickname, "Mamba," for the deadly Black Mamba snake. In a truly scary image that happily got little attention, he posed for a *Slam* magazine cover, caressing a black snake. He vented at everyone around him, even longtime loyalists like publicist John Black. Blaming him for failing to keep the press at bay, Bryant hired a personal publicist, whom Black was obliged to go through.

In a surprise, they started 23–11, with a boost from second-year center Andrew Bynum, but he was just 19 and hit the wall at midseason. Jackson asked Bryant to carry them again, but this wasn't the season before, with some hungry young guys who were getting it. Now some dizzy young guys were tuning out.

Kwame Brown, hurt again, shut it down until the playoffs, ignoring Jackson's pleas to play a few games at the end. Point guard Smush Parker, realizing he wouldn't be offered a new contract, pouted so badly that Jackson finally moved rookie Jordan Farmar ahead of him in the playoffs.

Bryant sagged under their weight. In an April 4 loss to the Clippers, he went 45 minutes, asking Jackson not to take him out for his normal rest at the end of the third quarter, and flamed out at the end.

Said Jackson, "He told me, 'We'd probably be 10 points behind before I took my first breath.' I said, 'You're probably right.'"

Jackson teams normally peaked at the end of the season. This one crashed, finishing 42–40, tied for No. 7 in the West. They met the Suns again but were run over in five games this time.

Bryant, who had smoldered for weeks, announced his dissatisfaction afterward, in the first complaint he had uttered in the three years since Shaquille O'Neal left. "Personally, for me, it's beyond frustration—three years and still being at ground zero," he said. "This summer's a big summer. We have to see what direction we want to take as an organization and make those steps and make them now."

★ ★ ★

If the Lakers thought that was bad, they hadn't seen anything yet.

All the bad off-seasons in their history, like 2004 when they thought they might lose Shaq and Kobe, and all the feuds, like Wilt and Butch van Breda Kolff, were warm-up acts compared to what was coming.

Four weeks after their last game, when Bryant had put the organization on notice in a professional manner, things only looked bleaker. Odom and Brown had undergone surgery, making any deals involving them difficult. The draft had sent super-prospect Greg Oden to the rebuilding Portland Trail Blazers.

Asked if he still felt as he had, Bryant mildly restated his position to Mike Bresnahan of the

*Once cool with officials, Bryant becomes a perennial leader in technical fouls.*

*Los Angeles Times*: "I'm still frustrated. I'm waiting for them to make some changes."

The story ran May 27, alongside columns by Bill Plaschke ("It's time to trade Bryant") and T.J. Simers ("Bryant's whine is more like sour grapes").

Stung, Bryant called ESPN's Ric Bucher to suggest the Lakers rehire Jerry West, retired again after five years as Memphis GM. Paraphrasing what Kobe had told him—Bucher got the call on his cell while driving and couldn't take notes—he went on the air and quoted Kobe as saying, "Short of doing that, yes, I have a no-trade clause. Yes, I'd be willing to waive that. You might as well go ahead and trade me because I can't wait for the current team to develop."

For two days Bryant claimed he didn't say he wanted to be traded, until erupting after another *Times* columnist—me—quoted a "Laker insider," as saying Kobe was responsible for this mess in the first place.

The reference ran deep in the column, in the following passage:

> Bryant has been a perfect organization man for three seasons, maintaining a steadfast belief in the same goal they pursued, however unrealistic it was.
>
> Nevertheless, as a Laker insider notes, it was Bryant's insistence on getting away from O'Neal that got them into this mess.

Concluding the "insider" was Buss, his son Jim, or John Black, a fuming Bryant went on the radio with ESPN's Stephen A. Smith, demanding to be traded. Then Kobe went back on with Dan

Patrick, whose show was up next, softening his stance and reversing his position to the pro-Laker *Loose Cannons* show on XTRA Sports Radio in Los Angeles, before repeating his trade demand to Bresnahan at the *Times*.

Bryant now saw lies and betrayal in everything the Lakers had done since trading O'Neal, from telling him they wouldn't rebuild to refusing to trade Bynum for Jason Kidd. When Buss issued a mild prepared statement, noting that Kobe hadn't actually told them he wanted to be traded, Bryant railed about it to the *Boston Globe*'s Jackie MacMullan:

> Unbelievable. I called Mitch Kupchak…to give him a heads-up, to let him know I was going to say I wanted to be traded. That seemed like the right thing to do. So don't act all surprised when the news comes out.…
>
> The Lakers have been watching me get killed in the media for the past three years. They've sat by and watched me get crucified, and they've done nothing to help me. I've rolled with it up to this point.
>
> No more.…
>
> I've heard nothing from him, but then here comes this statement that has Jerry Buss trying to make me sound unprofessional. That statement was extremely telling to me. It tells me all I need to know about Jerry Buss.

Actually, Buss had always had Bryant's back, insisting from the moment that he traded

*After Phoenix runs Los Angeles over in the '07 first round, Bryant informs the Lakers that he's had it, declaring, "Do something. Do it now."*

O'Neal that it was his decision alone, he did it for financial reasons, and Bryant had nothing to do with it. Rebuilding was so far from Buss' mind, Tomjanovich jokingly called it "the *R* word."

It was no longer about reason. It was about Bryant being stuck in L.A. The pièce de résistance came in a video shot by three fans in a parking lot outside the Newport Coast Shopping Center, where they approached Bryant, pleading with him to stay.

When Bryant began ranting at length, one of them began shooting.

"Andrew Bynum, what the fuck, are you kidding me?" says Bryant, his voice rising.

"He's the one who drafted Bynum so he doesn't want to let him go," says one of the fans, alluding to Kupchak.

"Fucking ship his ass out!" squeals Bryant. "C'mon, Jason Kidd? Why wouldn't you want to do that? Now we sit here in this fucked up position.... You know what, man? Let me just say something, Mitch Kupchak had the nerve to ask me…"

The rest was inaudible as the 32-second snippet ran out. The fans said Bryant's full statement was: "Mitch Kupchak had the nerve to ask me, 'How good do you think Andrew Bynum is going to be in 10 years?' Are you fucking kidding me? I'm trying to win this shit now!"

Bryant may or may not have known he was being filmed, but, as a Laker official noted, he also posed for a picture with the fans, presumably taken with the same device. In keeping with the theater-of-the-absurd atmosphere, the fans then went into business as the Kobe Video Guys, offering the video to the Lakers—reportedly noting they would make it public otherwise. Fortunately for the young entrepreneurs, the team

was busy or it might have turned the matter over to the LAPD.

The Kobe Video Guys then approached press outlets from coast to coast. "This video is

GOLD," they wrote in an e-mail to the *Times'* Bresnahan. "We were offered up to $10K for it last week by ABC, which was going to run it on ESPN."

With no actual offers, they finally sold it on the Internet at $1.99 a download, taunting Bresnahan: "It aired all right, you could have broke the story, but instead you choose to be paranoid."

*For owner Jerry Buss, whose stars had always adored him for his generosity, Bryant's rage was devastating.*

It was a new low for Bryant. Until then, his disasters had at least been understandable for one who had gotten so much so soon. He had been young and in love when he broke with his family over Vanessa. He hadn't properly appreciated what he had with O'Neal, but neither had Shaq.

This controversy, however, he had created out of thin air, with no more provocation than other stars stuck on bad teams—like Allen Iverson in Philadelphia, Kevin Garnett in Minnesota, and Paul Pierce in Boston—had handled gracefully for years. Bryant, meanwhile, got so much air time he eclipsed the ongoing postseason. Wrote the *Dallas Morning News'* David Moore after the Spurs eliminated Utah in the Western Conference Finals:

> The San Antonio Spurs have returned to the Finals. This ranks as the NBA's fifth-biggest story, behind Kobe's desire to be traded, Kobe's hurt feelings, Kobe's indecision, and Kobe's declaration that he wants to be a Laker for life.
>
> Luckily, no one asked Kobe Bryant whom he would have chosen to replace Paul Wolfowitz at the World Bank. Otherwise, the Spurs wouldn't have cracked the top five.

Two weeks later, Buss, who had had only one brief telephone conversation with Bryant, took a side trip to Barcelona on his annual European trip, to meet Kobe, who was there with his family.

Nothing Buss said could move Bryant, who repeated his demand to be traded. For emphasis, Kobe posted it on his website, saying good-bye to Laker fans as if he were already gone:

The Lakers are pursuing a longer-term plan that is different from what Dr. Buss shared with me at the time I re-signed as a free agent. I have seen that plan unfold for the last three years and watched great trade opportunities come and go and have seen free agents passed on. That has led to the Lakers not winning a playoff series. All of that was frustrating in itself, but then...to have someone "inside" the Laker organization try to blame me in the media

for us not being a contender right now—that is what brought me to my current position today.

I want it to be clear that I still love, with all my heart, the Laker Legacy. From Mikan to West to Goodrich to Wilt to Kareem to Magic. That will never change. And the support my family and I have gotten from Lakers fans is undeniably the best. But now there is a new road ahead. I am gonna keep grindin' and keep workin' to get back to competing for championships. Sometimes the trek up the mountain is tough. But I know we'll get there.

Strength and Honor,

Kobe

Bryant got "Strength and Honor" from General Maximus Decimus Meridius in the movie *Gladiator*. In Kobe's case, the strength was undeniable, but the honor was now not only arguable but portable.

*GM Mitch Kupchak, designated scapegoat, works on his next move.*

# Born Again

Few teams ever had an off-season as bad as the Lakers in the summer of 2007 or a season as surprising as the one that followed. Absolutely no one ever had both.

One moment they were staring into the abyss, with Kobe Bryant cursing their name, from owner Jerry Buss down, and demanding a trade, which Buss agreed to pursue. The next moment they were not only back, but they were also one of the NBA's brightest young teams. You had to see it to believe it, and even then, if you remembered back to the start, it was incomprehensible.

But it happened. You can look it up.

*Being Kobe Bryant: It's never over 'til it's over—even when it looks like it's over.*

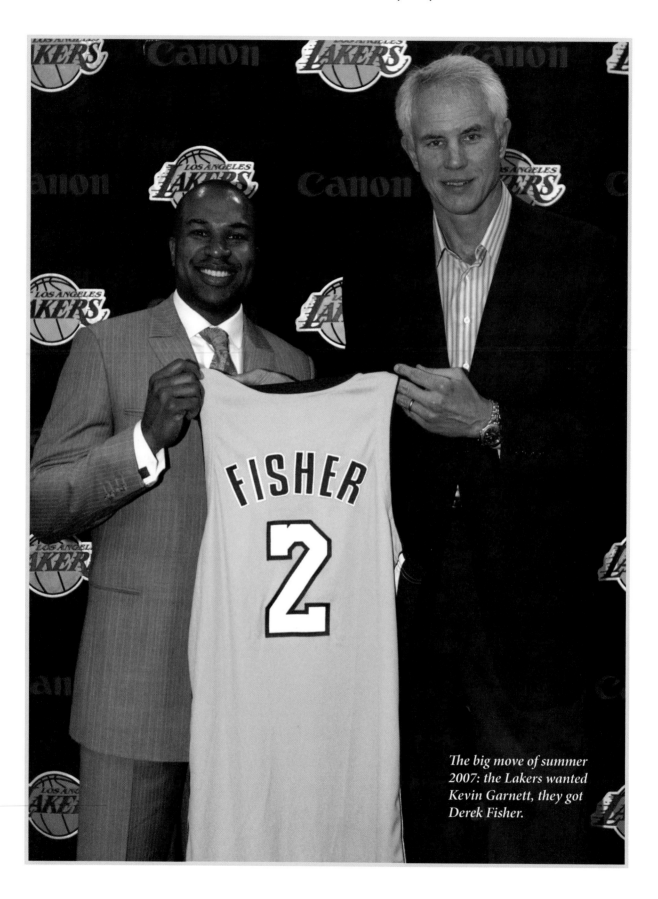

*The big move of summer 2007: the Lakers wanted Kevin Garnett, they got Derek Fisher.*

* * *

Bryant's days of rage finally blew out in the spring of 2007, allowing Laker officials to come back out, as if emerging from a bunker after an air bombardment.

As mad as Kobe was, the team controlled the situation. With two years before he could opt out, they didn't have to trade him.

In Barcelona, Bryant and Buss agreed to keep further dealings out of the press. Kobe stopped talking about it—publicly—but fumed on. In Las Vegas, where he joined the U.S. team in July as it prepared to qualify for the Olympics, ESPN's Ric Bucher reported flatly that Kobe would "never wear a Laker uniform again."

Bucher filed many such reports in the following months, as did other Kobe confidants, like Stephen A. Smith. Nothing the Lakers did could mollify Bryant, who even reacted stonily to speculation they would land Kevin Garnett. With the whole league bidding on KG, the Lakers made arguably the best offer—Andrew Bynum and Lamar Odom—but Minnesota boss Kevin McHale sent his star to Boston for Al Jefferson, Ryan Gomes, Sebastian Telfair, Gerald Green, and a No. 1 pick. Everyone else muttered that McHale, the former Celtic great, had given his old team a sweetheart deal, but, for the Lakers, it looked like their last hope to keep Bryant had sailed away.

The Lakers' only move was re-signing Derek Fisher, an old Bryant favorite. No matter how much Kobe loved Fish, this mess was bigger than that.

No Laker player, coach, or official even knew if Bryant would report to camp. Kobe let the suspense build until the end but turned up on time for media day. Correct, if not bubbly, he acknowledged he had been angry but insisted, "The important thing for everybody to understand is, I want to bring a title back to L.A."

The Lakers then jetted off to Honolulu for 10 days. It would take more than swaying palms and ocean breezes to get past this, but Bryant was constructive on the floor and relaxed off it, spotted around town with teammates more than ever before.

Then Buss did his sit-down with the beat writers, an annual session to make up for the fact that the flamboyant owner, who was actually media-shy and soft-spoken, would duck them the rest of the season. Buss normally said little, but he made up for it this time, not only declaring that Bryant was available but sounding as if he had already cut his ties to Kobe. "You can't keep too many loyalties," Buss said. "You've got to look at it as a business. He looks at it the same way I look at it."

For Buss, everything had changed in the meeting with Bryant in Barcelona in July, where, he said, Kobe had been implacable.

"He listened very carefully for 30, 45 minutes," said Buss. "I tried to explain to him how much the city of Los Angeles loved him and that to leave 10 million sweethearts for unknown territory might not be the right thing to do. But when I was finished, he said he basically felt the same way.

"And I said, 'Okay. With that, I will proceed to see what's available.'"

So much for the line that Bryant would not be traded, which the team had stuck to all summer. This dispute was new for Buss, who had always doted on his stars and had never had one who was unhappy, much less angry at him.

Laker staffers insisted the owner's remarks didn't contain anything new, but the man they had to convince—Bryant—wasn't going for it, putting out a steely prepared statement: "Dr. Buss' comments today provided more insight to a conversation we shared in Barcelona earlier this summer. I have touched on this conversation and other conversations within the Lakers' organization during the recent months and again at the Lakers' media day. I have nothing further to add and look forward to the upcoming season with my teammates."

What Bryant meant was:

*We agreed to keep this between us, and you can't even do that.*

⋆ ⋆ ⋆

Now it was like trying to put Humpty Dumpty back together after he fell out of an airplane.

Back from Hawaii for the exhibition season, Bryant renewed his demand to be traded. Certain that Kupchak hadn't really been trying, Kobe and his agent, Rob Pelinka, asked for and received permission to talk directly to other teams.

Bryant's choice was Chicago, a major market in the junior-varsity East, where LeBron James had just taken the rag-tag Cleveland Cavaliers to the Finals. Pelinka began talking to Bulls GM John Paxson, but it was slow going. The Bulls had a lot of young players but not enough to split into a package that would satisfy the Lakers, with enough left in Chicago to satisfy Bryant.

The Bulls didn't want to give up Luol Deng. The Lakers said they needed someone even better,

who had been an All-Star. The Bulls tried to get one from a third team—Ron Artest, whom Jackson had always liked—offering Ben Gordon to Sacramento. Kings GM Geoff Petrie said no.

Meanwhile, with several of its people close to Bryant, ESPN's *SportsCenter* reported imminent deals nightly. ESPN2's *Cold Pizza* was so sure the deal was going down one night, it invited the *Chicago Tribune*'s Sam Smith to come on at 6:30 the next morning. Smith, who was plugged into the Bulls, as opposed to getting information from Pelinka, declined, knowing nothing was going on.

At camp in El Segundo, the Lakers hung on by their fingernails, as Bryant skipped practice for three days—to rest a sore knee, Jackson said. The real story was that even if Bryant wasn't gone, Jackson was preparing for the possibility he would be.

"It was just like, are we going to have to learn how to play without Kobe, or are we going to play with him?" Jackson said later. "At this point, he had tendinitis. Might as well sit him out, and we'll go through this period of time.

"The players were questioning what was going to happen. They were upset. I didn't think they'd be upset, but I had to address them as a whole to say, 'We have to go on with what we do in a professional manner, regardless of what's going on at this period of time. And none of us can resolve this ourselves. There's nothing we can do about it. This is in the cards, or it's sitting in hands beyond ours.'"

⋆ ⋆ ⋆

With trade talks stymied, Bryant reluctantly concluded he was stuck with the Lakers—for the moment—and returned to practice the day before the opener.

People who weren't using superstar logic—*I want what I want when I want it*—had known all along how hard a trade would be on the eve of the season when everyone was optimistic, or had fallen for their own BS, and deals were rare. By the trade deadline in February, reality would have set in, and more would be possible.

Back for who-knew-how-many months, Bryant went on a charm offensive so sweet he almost glazed the Laker press corps. No matter how shaken he had looked after Buss' comments, he was fine. ("I'm playing like crap, but I'm fine"). He was aware of trade talks but wasn't involved and didn't know if Pelinka was ("Ask Rob"). He couldn't say he'd be here all season ("I'm not Nostradamus") but was

*In the never-to-be-forgotten 2007 opener, some Laker fans boo Kobe, some beg him to stay.*

committed to his teammates ("We're a close-knit group").

Pelinka and the Bulls were still talking, but they were out of ideas. As alarmed as Paxson was that trade stories were distracting his young team, it would be three more days before he held a press conference to announce, "There's no deal to be done."

On October 30, the Lakers opened at home against Houston, and Bryant was booed upon introduction. It wasn't arena-wide, but it wasn't hard to hear, either. Coming from the Lakers' truest believers, it was like seeing the Pope booed in St. Peter's Basilica. In a game appropriate to the crestfallen mood, the Lakers lost 95–93. Bryant missed 19 of his first 29 shots but scored 18 points in the fourth quarter as they came from 10 down in the last 2:30 to tie it, before Shane Battier punctured the moment, winning it with a three-pointer with :02 left.

Stung by the boos, Bryant said, "I understand where they're coming from, but they really don't know the entire situation. I'll just keep my mouth shut—as I should."

In other words, he hadn't done anything wrong. In his mind, the whole thing was still on the Lakers. When Bryant chose a path of action, nothing could turn him, and his path now led to the gates of Lakerdom. If Buss already despaired of changing Kobe's mind, opening night confirmed the owner's worst fears.

★ ★ ★

Happily, the Lakers had two days off before their second game, in Phoenix, against their nemesis. In the first of many surprises, they massacred the Suns 119–98, with Bynum getting 14 points and 13 rebounds off the bench.

It began to seem like an NBA season, rather than a death spiral, but beneath the surface nothing had changed. On ESPN's telecast of the Lakers' November 16 win over Detroit, Bucher reported that Bryant was still intent on leaving.

Then something totally unexpected happened—the Lakers became good, winning 17 of 20, with Bynum becoming a force. An apt student, tutored by Kareem Abdul-Jabbar, Andrew at 20 was twice as good as Kwame Brown, whose indifference made up for his million-dollar body. Jackson clung to Kwame because he was strong enough to push centers off the block and nimble enough to switch on pick-and-rolls, noting, "With Kwame, you can have a predictable defense."

As it turned out, with Bynum, long shot that he was, they could have a future.

In high school in Metuchen, New Jersey, Andrew had been blubbery and unfocused, playing two half-seasons after transferring. A late move in his senior year got him invited to the prestigious McDonald's game, but UConn, which had signed him, still had him slated to back up Josh Boone and Hilton Armstrong. When the Lakers drafted Bynum, his high school coach was incredulous, noting their brief stay in the state tournament, asking, "If he's an NBA player, how do I lose in the first round?"

That draft would became a signature moment for Laker management in the dark spring of 2005, when a season-ticket holder asked GM Mitch Kupchak to resign, and fans were dismayed to hear Buss talking of turning over duties to his son

*The game in which everything turned: the Lakers upset the Suns in Phoenix in the second game in 2007.*

Jim. Of Jerry's four children by his wife, Joanne, only Jeannie had graduated from college and gone to work. The oldest, John, raced cars. Jim trained horses before assuming a ceremonial title as assistant general manger. As opposed to studying under past GM Jerry West, Jim once told *Sports Illustrated*'s Franz Lidz, "If you grabbed 10 fans out of a bar and asked them to rate prospects, their opinions would be pretty much identical to those of the pro scouts."

As far as Laker fans were concerned, it was as if Jed Clampett had handed over the *Beverly Hillbillies* to his nephew, Jethro.

Buss, the swashbuckling gambler who had always gone for broke, had also begun saving for the estate tax his children would inherit with the team. Jackson, who had an impeccable source, shared Bryant's concerns about the owner's commitment.

No one had thought much of Bynum in the McDonald's game, but he looked better in a workout in New York several weeks later after trimming off 20 pounds. Laker assistant GM Ronnie Lester, who attended, told Kupchak they should take another look. The Lakers arranged a private workout at the predraft camp in Chicago, and Kupchak, knowing he would need help to get the owner to take a high school kid, invited Jim, who caught the fever with the rest of the staff.

Jackson wanted someone a little further beyond puberty, Arizona's Channing Frye. Kupchak promised to take Frye if he was there, but he wasn't, going to New York two picks before at No. 8. That freed Kupchak to take Bynum at No. 10, four months shy of 18, the youngest NBA player ever.

Bynum played little as a rookie but improved enough in his second season to bring offers pouring in. By Thanksgiving of this season, Andrew's third, Jackson sent Brown to the bench to stay.

The Lakers spurted to a 26–11 start, but Bryant remained somber and detached. On Christmas, Bynum scored 28 points as they routed the Suns again. Phoenix coach Mike D'Antoni, when asked if Andrew was up and coming, said, laughing, "He's there. The guy's 11-for-13. I hope he's not up and coming."

Said Bryant stonily, "I'm focused on one thing and one thing only. That's winning a championship. I could care less about what happens Christmas Day."

Two weeks into January, Bynum was averaging 19 points and 13 rebounds for the month, when he was lost with a knee injury. The next night, the Lakers won in Seattle, and Bryant sent his best wishes to Bynum in the normally banal courtside interview, then uttered the 10 words that changed everything:

"We're a championship-caliber team with him in the lineup."

*We?*

Without fanfare, Bryant was back. After days of rage, weeks of intrigue, and months of alienation, Kobe was like Dorothy returning from Oz, sighing, "There's no place like home."

Showing how much things had changed, karmic as well as real, Kupchak now renewed his pursuit of Memphis' Pau Gasol—and landed him. The Grizzlies, out to dump Pau's $15 million salary, handed him over for Brown, Javaris Crittenton, Aaron McKie, two first-round draft picks, and the rights to Marc Gasol. The key was

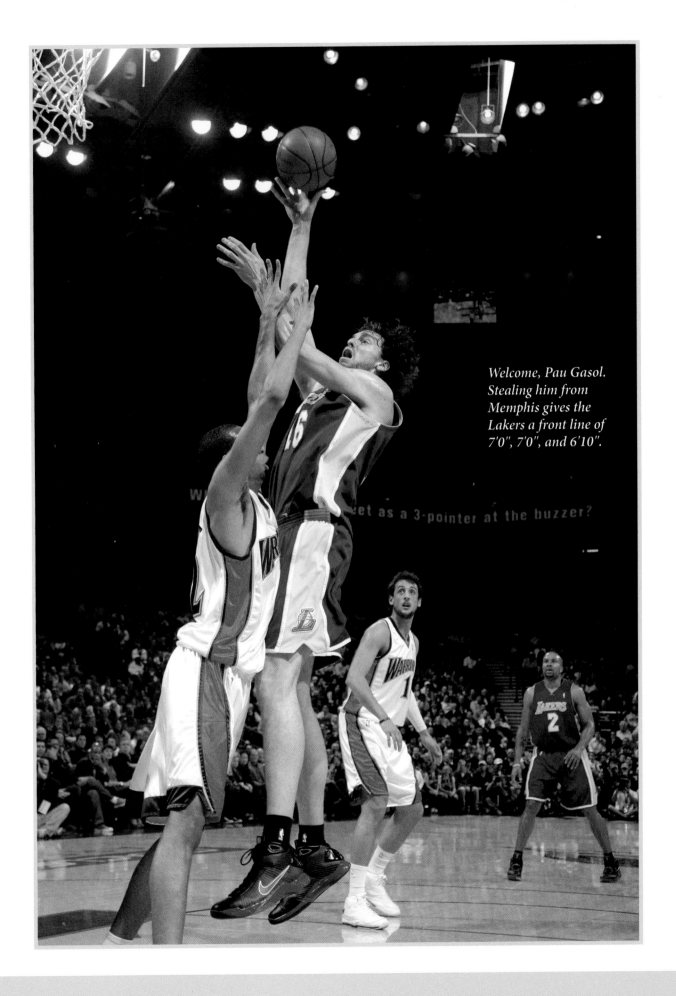

*Welcome, Pau Gasol. Stealing him from Memphis gives the Lakers a front line of 7'0", 7'0", and 6'10".*

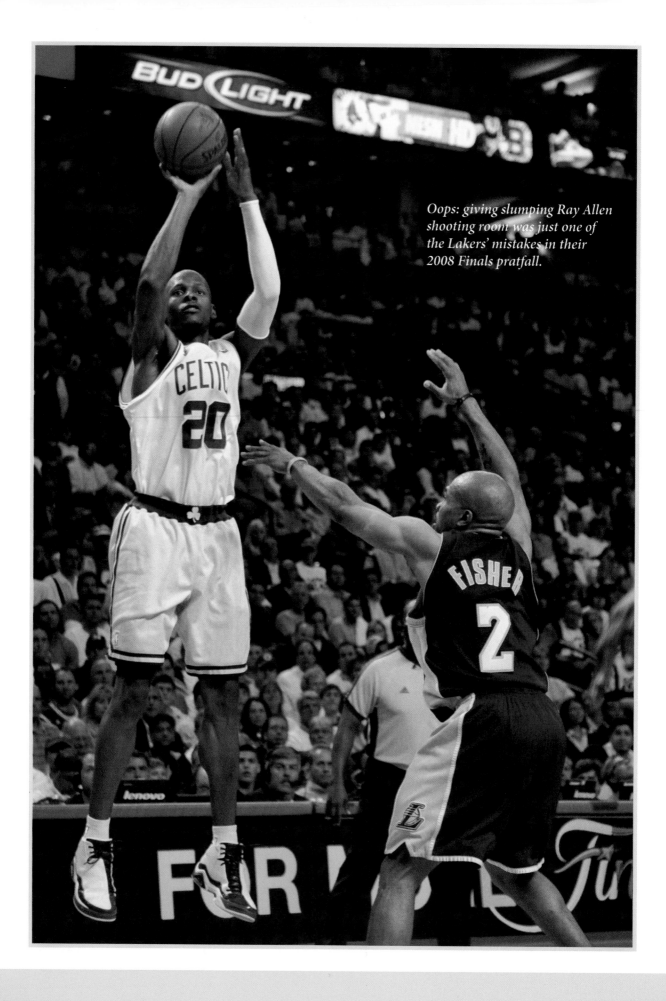

*Oops: giving slumping Ray Allen shooting room was just one of the Lakers' mistakes in their 2008 Finals pratfall.*

Buss' willingness to take on Pau Gasol's contract, which ran three more seasons—exposing the Lakers to a potential $90 million in extra salary and luxury tax.

An effusive Bryant apologized publicly to Kupchak for ever doubting him. The next time he was asked about their differences, Kobe said, "Good thing I wasn't the GM."

The Lakers went 22–5 with Gasol in the lineup, and finished 57–25, No. 1 in the West. As if the gods were trying to squeeze all the irony they could out of this, Bryant, who had looked stark raving mad the summer before, won his first MVP.

Not that it was an important step for him, but ESPNews anchor David Lloyd, watching Bryant joke with teammates at the announcement, mused, "I don't think I knew that Kobe was a well-liked guy on that team until this press conference.... He's become a part of that team. I'm not sure he was before."

★ ★ ★

A funny thing happened in the last chapter of their storybook season. It turned out to be someone else's storybook season.

With Bynum's return pushed back and finally called off, the Lakers still went 12–3 in the West draw, zooming into the Finals against Boston. It was as if both of their histories had come full circle, recalling the Laker wins over the Celtics in the last two meetings (as the Lakers liked to think of it), after years of domination, with Boston winning the first eight (as the Celtics liked to think of it).

As if sounding an old call to arms, Celtic owner Wyc Grousbeck, who had been there five years,

assuming the mantle of Red Auerbach, exulted, "And we're 8–2!" That was the Shot Heard 'Round Lakerdom. Even Jerry West, retired and living in Malibu, bristled, saying "He was also the same owner who saw his team not make the playoffs."

The Celtics hadn't reached the Finals in 21 years and hadn't even been in the playoffs in eight of the last 12. With the newly acquired Garnett and Ray Allen, they had posted the NBA's best record, 66–16, but then gone seven games in the first round against Atlanta, seven in the second against Cleveland, and six in the Eastern Conference Finals against Detroit.

Unfortunately for the Lakers, now up to 34–8 with Gasol in the lineup, this didn't turn out like the '80s, when their edge in talent and youth prevailed. This was more like the '60s, when Bill Russell's giant shadow loomed over them. Now, as then, the Celtics won on defense with a beautifully coordinated scheme, designed by coach Doc Rivers' assistant, Tom Thibodeau. With Garnett dropping off Odom to jam up the middle and physical Kendrick Perkins containing Gasol one-on-one, that left three Celtics tracking Bryant.

Worse, the Lakers flashed a blithe confidence before Games 1 and 2, suggesting they thought they had the situation in hand. Meanwhile, the Celtics' hunger bordered on desperation.

Boston won Game 1 98–88, as Bryant shot 9-for-26, insisting he missed a bunch of "bunnies." Unfazed, Jackson joked about Paul Pierce's exit by wheelchair after hurting his knee, with Pierce returning minutes later and knocking down back-to-back three-pointers.

Pierce's return prompted Willis Reed comparisons throughout New England. Jackson, who had been Reed's teammate when Willis dragged his numb leg out for Game 7 of the 1970 Finals, knew it wasn't quite the same. Being Phil Jackson, he said it.

"I don't know what was going on there, was Oral Roberts back in their locker room?" said Jackson before Game 2, breaking up the interview room.

For his part, when Bryant was asked about the "Paul Pierce drama," he laughed.

"Phil was skeptical?" said Doc Rivers in mock disbelief. "Oh, I don't care. Aren't we skeptics anyway now about everything? So what the heck? Let it begin. Let it begin. Lee Harvey Oswald did it."

Let what begin? This was going one way—Boston's. Game 2 was a rout until the fourth quarter when the Lakers cut a 24-point deficit to four but still lost 108–102. Pierce got 28. The Lakers stopped making whimsical comments.

Back in Staples Center, the Lakers eked out an 87–81 win in Game 3. Bryant, abandoning the offense, scored 36 points, getting into the lane often enough to shoot 18 free throws.

In Game 4, the Lakers finally cracked Boston's defense with magical ball movement, going up by 24 in the third quarter—when the Celtics began grinding their way back. Bryant, who was 0–4 in the first half, tried to take over, but against this defense, in which good looks were so hard to get, he couldn't turn it on and off. In the most devastating Laker loss since the 1985 Memorial Day Massacre, the Celtics won 97–91.

The Lakers won Game 5 to send it back to Boston but needn't have bothered. Bryant scored 11 points in the first 6:30 of Game 6, but the roof fell in as soon as he tried to involve teammates.

*Paul Pierce left Game 1 in a wheelchair but went home for the summer with the Finals MVP trophy.*

The Celtics turned the humiliation up to full tilt, treating the Lakers like punks in a 131–92 thrashing.

Finals appearance or no Finals appearance, MVP or no MVP, it was like the last three seasons when people either said Bryant shot too much or not enough. The first question in the interview room was: "We've seen you do the impossible, 30 points in a quarter, 81 in one game.... When did you sort of concede that tonight you guys weren't going to be able to come out of the hole?"

*Sort of concede?*

A glowering Bryant answered tonelessly, ignoring the insult and the question, as well as the questions that followed: "Not sure. I don't know."

★ ★ ★

Some years, ignominy isn't so ignominious. Despite their fall, the Lakers had started out contemplating their destruction and wound up playing for a title.

"I'm comfortable with what we have," said Bryant a few days later. "It's more of a relaxing summer for me because I know we have an opportunity to win....

"It's funny how life works out, man, and how things can turn pretty quickly and for the better....You know me, I'm eternally optimistic."

Bryant was actually a lot of things but, happily for the Lakers, at least he was still theirs.

The Celtic Curse surfaces again.

*What, them worry? Trevor Ariza, Bynum, Bryant, and Fisher break up on the bench during a Lakers rout.*

# They're Back

*We have met the enemy, and he is us.*

—from *Pogo* by Walt Kelly

Nothing could stand in the Lakers' way now. At least, that was the way it seemed to everyone, including the Lakers.

It wasn't often that an NBA finalist came back with a new 7'0" center capable of averaging 13 points and 10.0 rebounds, as Andrew Bynum had in the first half of the preceding season. Beyond that, the Lakers were on a mission. They had been humbled. They had learned a bitter lesson at the hands of their archrivals.

That was their story, anyway, and they were sticking with it.

★ ★ ★

Media day, which had seen so much drama in recent years, was like a walk in a meadow, with nary an issue, and no national press hanging on every word.

"It's amazing what can happen in just a year's time on and off the court," said a bemused Derek Fisher. "I'm sure the Celtics training camp is buzzing quite a bit. There may be some other training camps that may be buzzing with more of a national presence, but we love you guys just as much. We'll take our home cooking, and we'll keep it moving for now."

When the Lakers started 7–0, local optimism zoomed off the charts, as talk shows rang with 70-win predictions. Unfortunately, the Lakers already looked bored, carrying bad team after bad team into the fourth quarter before wearing opponents down with sheer numbers, with reserves Lamar Odom, Trevor Ariza, Jordan Farmar, and Sasha Vujacic now known as the "Bench Mob."

Coach Phil Jackson seemed unconcerned. After they hung on to beat an eight-man Phoenix squad 115–110, someone asked if he had noticed he was saying the same thing after every game—they had played okay, Pau Gasol had been great, but nobody else had stood out.

Said Jackson, straight-faced: "You know, I thought Fish played very well. Maybe I should mention that. His defense was solid. He made some steals. I like that."

"But do you sense repetition in these games, as you talk about them afterward?" a reporter asked.

"Maybe I'll put it on tape and just run it right here on the podium, so you guys don't have to ask me questions," said Jackson, grinning.

The Lakers said they were just inconsistent, but they were consistency itself. Compared to the all-heart Celtics, who would win 27 of their first 29, and the hard-nosed Cavaliers, who were right on Boston's tail, the Lakers didn't play very hard.

That was hardly unknown in Lakerdom, where Shaquille O'Neal once used the regular season to get in shape. Now, however, with Shaq gone and the soap opera days over, the Lakers seemed to have a new sense of entitlement to go with the new harmony. Jackson was taking it easy on his young players, more concerned with having five of them who were 25 or younger in rotation. The ferocious Bryant and the hard-nosed Fisher were taking their cues from Phil.

Jackson's easy-rider approach had worked marvelously in Chicago, where he had to hold Michael Jordan and Co. back, and then again when he won three titles under completely different circumstances, with Shaq and Kobe fencing until spring, then joining hands and running over anyone in their way.

This Laker team wasn't as good as those teams, but it still had things well in hand by the All-Star break. For the second season in a row they lost Bynum to a knee injury in January, and for the second season in a row, they showed they could play without him, winning 11 of the next 12, including upsets in Boston and Cleveland on their big East Coast trip, giving them season sweeps over the Celtics and Cavaliers.

After that, the Lakers had two months to play out the string. With the Spurs, Hornets, Mavericks, and Suns in decline and no one else coming out of the pack in the West, they won the conference by 11 games. Unlike the season before, Bynum made it back, playing the last four games, averaging 17 points in 26 minutes.

*Being Phil Jackson: no matter how ragged his young team got, he had it covered, he thought.*

*Hungering for revenge all summer, the Lakers beat the Celtics in the Staples Center on Christmas Day.*

Their long wait for the postseason was over. Even with LeBron James spurring the Cavaliers to the NBA's best record, 66–16 to their 65–17, the Lakers were favorites once more and a cinch to come out of the West.

What could go wrong now?

★ ★ ★

The Lakers dispatched the Jazz 4–1 in the first round, but it was nothing like their 4–0 cakewalk over Denver the year before, when the Nuggets' bus caught fire on the way to the opener.

With the reeling Jazz losing seven of its last nine, including the finale to the Lakers, the hard-nosed Utah coach, Jerry Sloan, tried shock therapy, terming their chances "pretty bleak." Proving Sloan correct, his team lost Game 1 in Staples 113–100.

The Lakers were still so sloppy that Jackson, who counted down from 16 wins on the whiteboard in their dressing room, wrote: "15? Not like that." It turned out to be "15, even worse." The Lakers won Game 2 119–109 but let the Jazz cut a 20-point deficit to three. Beginning a string of excuses, Jackson blamed himself for playing his bench, which was no longer a weapon, too much.

In Game 3, Utah wiped out all of a 13-point Lakers lead and won 88–86 on Deron Williams' jumper with :02 left. Jackson, no longer bemused, shook up his lineup, benching Bynum, whose eight weeks off was showing. Andrew said nothing, but his people were frantic, with his agent, David Lee, calling GM Mitch Kupchak—and several press people—to register his anguish.

With Bryant leaving playmaker mode and coming out firing, 38 points worth, the Lakers won Game 4 108–94.

*The Jazz is tough but earthbound. The Lakers rule the skies in the first round.*

With Bynum struggling in the playoffs, the Lakers need the Gasol-Odom tandem that bombed in the '08 Finals. Surprise, it works!

Back in Staples, they finished off the Jazz 107–96, but not before letting a 22-point lead dwindle to three, forcing Jackson, who had taken his starters out, to rush them back in.

"You've got to give Utah credit," said Jackson. "We had a first-round opponent this year that was much tougher than last year.…This Utah team was not typically what you'd call an eighth-place team."

Nor had the Lakers looked like what you'd typically call a first-place team, although the worst was yet to come.

★ ★ ★

Unlike the Jazz, the Houston Rockets, the Lakers' second-round opponent, didn't come into their series in free fall. The Rockets, a tough defensive team, came to play, winning Game 1 in Staples 100–92.

Not that this alarmed the Lakers, as (yawn) usual. They had been off for a week, while the Rockets were coming off a tough six-game series with the Trail Blazers. Jackson would later note, "We weren't prepared for that first game," but what else was new? They rarely showed any urgency until someone slapped them across the face. After their Game 3 loss in Utah, Jackson had actually said Memo Okur's return from injury could help the Lakers, who needed "a lineup out there that challenges us and makes us play the way we should play."

Imagine how proud the Jazz must have been to finally field a lineup that got their attention.

Aroused, the Lakers were still formidable, as they showed, winning Game 2 111–98, then going

*You can't guard what you can't catch. Houston's Von Wafer zips around Andrew Bynum.*

to Houston to win Game 3 108–94. The Rockets then got the devastating news that Yao Ming was gone for the rest of the playoffs, which seemed to end that.

As if expecting the Rockets to ask for terms, the Lakers mailed one in, easing into Game 4 as the Rockets jumped to a 17–4 lead. With the Lakers confident the Rockets would start missing, Houston pushed it to 83–54 after three periods, with the pièce de résistance of Aaron Brooks laying in a lob on an inbounds play from halfcourt with :01 left in the quarter, over a shocked Farmar.

The Lakers lost just 99–87, but their humiliation was total—little as Jackson was inclined to admit it. Stung at being asked if he was embarrassed, he insisted he wasn't, noting before a live TV audience on ESPN:

"Houston played a great game. You should give them some fucking credit."

One wakeup call was a lot in the playoffs, when motivation was assumed everywhere else, and this was the Lakers' third in nine games. Railed ABC's Jeff Van Gundy during the telecast: "What are they thinking about? What do they care about?"

Said Laker co-owner and ABC commentator Magic Johnson: "I would have gone into my room and not come out for two or three days."

Jackson, worried less by the effort than at how his young players would handle being ripped, told them he was "dismayed" after Game 4 but continued to protect them in public.

"It's a different kind of group," said Fisher. "A lot of stock has been placed in Andrew and his potential at 21 years old—where, compared to

our teams in the past, the only guy near his early 20s who was being asked to do anything of major importance to us was Kobe.

"Now we're asking that of Trevor and Jordan and Andrew and Shannon [Brown], who's been here for two months—guy after guy, who are still trying to figure out where they fit in in this league, not to mention what their specific role is on this team.

"By the time we got to this level, Kobe and I were four-year guys, Shaq had been to the Finals and lost, and then we had Rick [Fox], and Rob [Horry], and Harp [Ron Harper]....You had thousands of NBA games experience and players who had been through everything."

The Lakers were just finding out how young these kids were, arriving ever younger, becoming famous sooner, making them inevitably dizzier.

Farmar had a blog on *Playboy*'s site, which became a must-read after he wrote about life at UCLA ("Groupies are always part of campus life, and it's something you have to watch out for. Girls used to come to our dorm room all the time, knocking on our door, leaving off notes and propositions.") Bynum hit the big time, celebrity-wise, when he was photographed with a Playboy bunny on his shoulders at a party at the mansion while the team was on the East Coast, in what didn't look like rehab.

Back in the starting lineup for Game 5, Bynum played his best game of the postseason, scoring 14 points with six rebounds as the Lakers flattened the Rockets 118–78. He then left without talking, while a team official fumed, part of a press boycott no one had even known about. The young center,

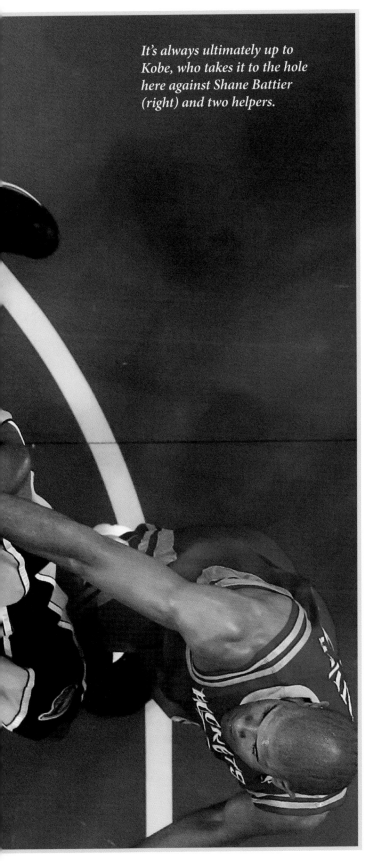

*It's always ultimately up to Kobe, who takes it to the hole here against Shane Battier (right) and two helpers.*

whose conduct had been exemplary, was copping his first attitude. As his mentor, Kareem Abdul-Jabbar, noted, "It'll benefit him so much to be accessible, but there's only so much influence I have."

The Lakers actually tried in Game 6 in Houston. The bad news was that that no longer guaranteed them anything, as they were drubbed again 95–80. By then, it had occurred to them that Houston had more going for it than Laker mood swings. The Lakers had more trouble guarding the Rockets' small lineup, especially 5'11", 160-pound Aaron Brooks, who was averaging 19 in the series.

Rising to yet another occasion…after letting yet another occasion develop…the Lakers arose to choke off Brooks in Game 7, shutting the Rockets down and winning easily 89–70. Free to say what he thought, when Bryant was asked what he had learned about his team, he eschewed the usual answer about their heart, courage, and so on, and said, "We're bipolar."

"There are no off-nights in the playoffs," announced Jackson, however belatedly. "Every night you want to compete….We just didn't do that in this series. We weren't prepared from the first game."

"We were stubborn," said Ariza. "We thought we could win on sheer talent."

The word Trevor was looking for wasn't *stubborn*, but *clueless*. They were still a work in progress—and they were behind schedule. With their season on the line in Game 7, Vujacic and Farmar got into a spat on the bench. By then, the coaches would have let them fight to the death if it wouldn't have left them shorthanded.

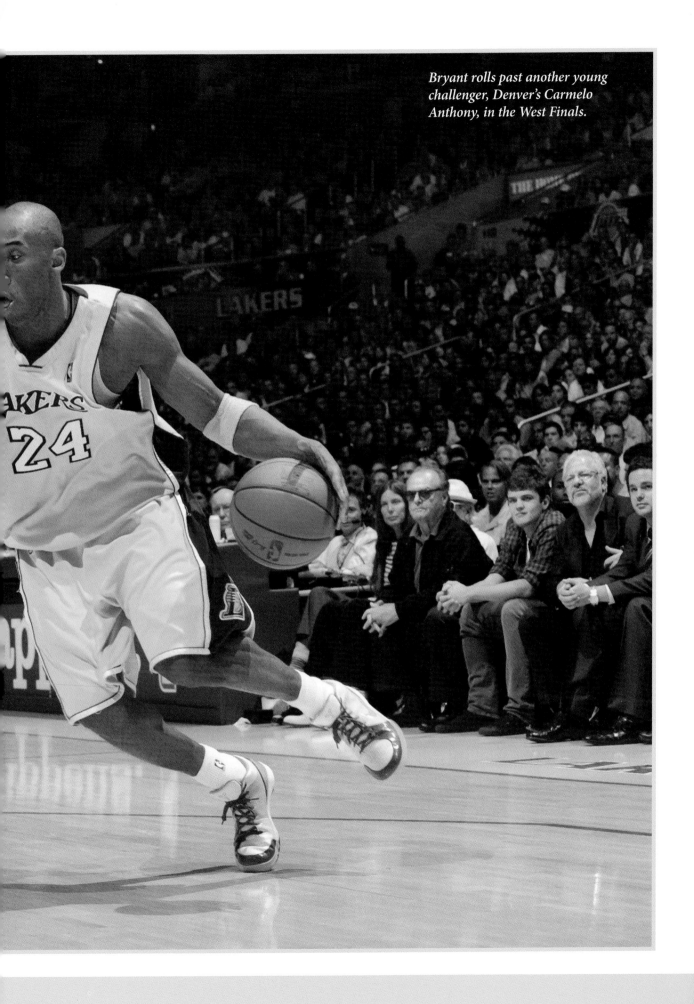

*Bryant rolls past another young challenger, Denver's Carmelo Anthony, in the West Finals.*

On the bright side, if losing to Boston the year before had been a learning experience, they were *really* learning their lesson this spring.

★ ★ ★

Happily for Jackson, who liked playing teams that got his players' attention, their next opponent, the Denver Nuggets, was the new trendy pick after storming through the first two rounds, going 8–2 against the Hornets and Mavericks.

"I'm absolutely done this year picking the Lakers," railed ABC's Mark Jackson during the Houston series. "I'm done. I'm picking the Denver Nuggets. I'm also going to pick the winner of the Eastern Conference, because one thing I know is those teams are going to show up. It's not going to be because they were outworked or gave a disappointing effort."

Bryant, asked about Jackson's comments on a talk radio show before the start of the Western Conference Finals, said: "Mark's right."

Effort, at least, was no longer an issue for the Lakers. This was fortunate, because with Bynum as a minor factor, they weren't close to their top end. The first three games were anyone's. The Lakers came from five behind in the last 4:30 to win Game 1. The Nuggets came from six behind in the last 14:33 to win Game 2.

In Denver for Game 3, the Lakers came from eight behind in the fourth quarter, taking home-court advantage back. Fighting exhaustion and double-teams, Bryant scored 41 points, eight in the last 1:30, including a remarkable three-pointer that put them ahead to stay, rising up over J.R. Smith, who ticked the ball on the way up—or Bryant's

hand, Kobe said. Bryant was so spent afterward he needed IV fluids.

Said Denver's George Karl, "I think Jesus would have trouble covering him."

The Nuggets wiped out the Lakers in Game 4, tying the series. At that point, with a few plays going the other way, the Lakers could have been up 3–1…or swept 4–0.

Everything changed in Game 5, back in Staples. With the Nuggets swarming over Bryant all series, Jackson now had Kobe bait them, holding the ball until the defenders committed, then finding his big men, Gasol, Bynum, and Odom. The Lakers won 103–94, with Gasol, Bynum, and Odom combining for 42 against the supposedly intimidating Nuggets, whose actual height across the front was 6'10" (Nene), 6'8" (Kenyon Martin), and 6'6½" (Carmelo Anthony).

The Lakers had them now. Back in Denver, the three Laker big men scored 42 more. When the Nuggets backed off Bryant, he attacked. The Lakers cruised 119–92.

Guess who was going back to the Finals after all?

★ ★ ★

Q: How do you not feel good about Game 1 so you don't come into Game 2 with a fat head?

A: Well, that's not an easy task, obviously…

—Phil Jackson,
after routing Orlando in Game 1

*Putting the Nuggets back in their place, the Lakers win in six games.*

*Andrew Bynum, now a part-timer and not happy about it, stews on the bench.*

And guess who wouldn't be there to greet them?

For weeks, the airwaves had hyped a Kobe-LeBron showdown. Vitaminwater, which both players endorsed, ran commercials debating who was best. Another sponsor, Nike, ran spots with Kobe and LeBron as puppets.

NBA Entertainment, Nike, and ESPN put out a documentary titled *Dream Season, 23 & 24,* a heartwarming story that started with Kobe and LeBron eying each other warily as teammates on the U.S. team, becoming friends, winning the Gold Medal in Beijing, and going home to lead their teams to a climactic duel. For the maraschino cherry atop the sundae of hubris, ESPN actually ran it after the Cavaliers were eliminated.

"As these friends grow closer to a showdown," mused narrator Justin Timberlake, "you have to wonder, what are they thinking?"

It wasn't hard to guess what LeBron was thinking. He felt like throwing one of his Nikes through his 60-inch flat screen.

The Cavaliers had been grinders all season, but exuberance reigned after their 8–0 romp in the first two rounds, with James leading pregame pantomimes in which they posed for a team picture as if they'd just won the title.

Inconveniently, they ran into a matchup problem in the Eastern Conference Finals. Orlando spread the floor with its sharpshooters, exposing the slow-footed Cleveland big men, who couldn't guard the perimeter or get back to lay a finger on Dwight Howard. The Magic won in six games, and if James hadn't won Game 2 with a last-second three, it would have been five.

Even while going 59–23, the Magic had been an afterthought, but it had a model inside-outside game that even the red-hot Cavaliers, with their rock-ribbed defense, couldn't get them out of. Remarkably for a young team, or showing how often it was overlooked, the Magic was at its best against the top teams, going

*If Orlando's Courtney Lee had made this layup to win Game 2, the Finals might have been different—but he didn't.*

17–9 against the Lakers, Cavaliers, and Celtics over two seasons, counting the playoffs. The only other member of the top four with a winning record against the others was Boston, at 16–15. The Lakers were 7–11.

More pratfalls could await if the Lakers got ahead of themselves again, but those days were over. Bryant ended them, personally, taking on a new baleful persona in the Finals. Being Kobe, he played it to the hilt, taking it into the interview room where he answered questions in as few words as possible, cracking a smile only when he acknowledged, "My kids are calling me *Grumpy*, from the Seven Dwarfs."

With that elusive fourth title tantalizingly within reach, nothing would stand in his way. No player as great as Bryant had ever shown as much zeal, and no one may have ever been as hungry as Kobe was now. On the floor, he often bared his teeth, jutting his jaw out for a truly scary look. "I just want it so bad, that's all," Bryant said. "I just want it so bad. You just put everything into the game, and your emotions flow out."

Of course, after the Lakers plowed the Magic under 100–75 in Game 1, everyone else was ready to hold the parade. Jackson dropped half his roster into Howard's lap, holding him to six shots, of which Dwight missed five. Bryant left rookie guard Courtney Lee to help on Howard, and the Magic shooters had gone cold.

Remarkably, Magic coach Stan Van Gundy regrouped his team in the two days before Game 2. The Magic still lost 101–96 in overtime but only after Lee missed a layup on an inbounds lob with :01 left in regulation, which Van Gundy had drawn up, knowing that Bryant, Lee's defender, would watch for a lob to Howard.

"Honestly, it was just a brilliant play," said Bryant. "It was a very, very smart play that he drew up. He knew my eye was more on the shooters coming up and just a hell of a play by a hell of a coach."

And his thoughts as he watched the pass soar over him?

"Shit," said Bryant, descriptively.

The Lakers were still up 2–0 going to Orlando, Howard had 29 points total, and point guard Rafer Alston was 3–17 from the floor. Nevertheless, the Magic turned back into its underrated, fearsome self in Game 3, shooting 76 percent in the first half and 63 percent overall—both Finals records—and won 108–104.

It seemed like the Denver series. Had Lee made that layup, the Magic would have been up 2–1, with two more at home to close it out, and the air seeming to leak out of the Lakers' soufflé. Their big men were capable of playing the game over opponents' heads, but Bynum had 18 points in three games and was in constant foul trouble against Howard.

The Magic came out hot again in Game 4, taking a 12-point lead at the half. The only thing hot about the Lakers was Jackson, the Yoda of coaches, who got a technical foul and complained of "bogus calls" in the sideline interview with ABC—for which he would be fined $25,000. The Lakers then stormed out of the dressing room and outscored the Magic 18–5, turning it back into a contest, but Orlando still led 87–84 with :10 left.

The Lakers inbounded the ball to Bryant, who was double-teamed in the backcourt and gave the ball up, which was all the Magic could hope for. The ball went to Ariza, then Fisher, who brought it up the right side as Orlando's Jameer Nelson

Kobe in Orlando, within sight
of the end of his long quest.

*Closing in, Bryant attacks the rim in Orlando.*

backpedaled—and then, stunningly, Fisher launched it, 26 feet out, a step behind the arc.

Aside from being 0–5 on threes to that point, Fisher rarely shot them off the dribble and almost never going to his right, as he was this time. At 34, his postseason had been agonizing, with Brooks torching him, prompting speculation he was through, after which he started pressing and went into a shooting slump. Even the supportive Laker bloggers had wondered why Jackson didn't bench him, or as one delicately phrased it during the Houston series, "Does loyalty play a part in your decisions of who starts?"

Nevertheless, Fisher was still the lion-hearted veteran who had stepped up one way or another his entire career. In 1998 as a 23-year-old backup to Nick Van Exel, with Bryant the only teammate younger, Fisher had been the one who tried to rally them during a crisis, writing all the players letters. In 2004, when Fisher lost his starting job to Gary Payton, he beat San Antonio with that famous 18-foot hook.

So it wasn't really that surprising that Fisher took this shot, or that he made it, tying the game 87–87. Or, if it was surprising, it was also poetic justice.

The Lakers won 99–91 in overtime, going ahead to stay with :31 left when Bryant got into the lane and pitched it back to Fisher, who knocked down one of his vintage spot-up threes.

There was no denying the Lakers in Game 5, even with the Magic taking a 19–10 lead, in a situation in which the Lakers had mailed it

*Little Mr. Big Shot: Fisher, who hit a storied shot against San Antonio in 2004, hits a bigger one against Orlando.*

in before. From that point to the middle of the fourth quarter, they outscored Orlando 75–48, cruising to a 99–86 win and their 15th NBA title.

A giddy Bryant, freed from years of hearing what he couldn't do without Shaq, admitted finally, "It was like Chinese water torture, just keep dropping a drop of water on your temple. I would cringe every time. I was just like, it's a challenge I'm just going to have to accept, because there's no way I'm going to argue it. You can say it until you're blue in the face and rationalize it until you're blue in the face, but it's not going anywhere until you do something about it."

For the crowning touch, with owner Jerry, son Jim, and daughter Jeannie Buss back home, one of the owner's younger sons, 25-year-old Joey, made his debut representing the Lakers, accepting the Larry O'Brien Trophy. With Celtics great Bill Russell, for whom the Finals MVP award was named, standing nearby, Joey gracelessly called out the Celtics, noting that the Lakers now trailed them in titles 17–15.

Of course, a year before, Celtics owner Wyc Grousbeck, who had been there for five mostly bad seasons, had reminded the Lakers that Boston still led them in Finals wins, crowing: "And we're 8–2!"

So maybe it was just payback.

In any case, it capped a memorable season for the Lakers, who needed one.

*The crowd that packed the 95,000-seat Coliseum cheers the Lakers.*

*The view at the top: Bryant with the championship trophy.*